CONNECTICUT
FARMER & FEAST

CONNECTICUT

FARMER & FEAST

Harvesting Local Bounty

EMILY BROOKS

gPP

GUILFORD, CONNECTICUT

All recipes developed by Emily Brooks, except for Whit Davis's Famous Johnny Cakes, used with permission of the Davis Family
Photos © Emily Brooks except those of Ms. Brooks on pages ix and 210 by Walter Kidd.
Map: Maryann Dube © Morris Book Publishing, LLC
Text design: Sheryl P. Kober
Project editor: Julie Marsh
Layout artist: Melissa Evarts

Library of Congress Cataloging-in-Publication Data

Brooks, Emily, 1975-
Connecticut farmer & feast : harvesting local bounty / Emily Brooks.
  p. cm.
 Includes index.
 ISBN 978-0-7627-6145-6
 1. Cooking (Natural foods) 2. Cooking—Connecticut. 3. Farms, Small—Connecticut. 4. Sustainable agriculture—
Connecticut. I. Title
TX741.B75 2011
641.59746—dc222010050684

Printed in China
10 9 8 7 6 5 4 3 2 1

This book is dedicated to Bill Brooks, without whom the dream of this book might not have ever been realized; the fearless Gladys Veidemanis, who valiantly dipped her manicured toes into the dangerous waters of sentence punctuation; Gretchen and Terry Bambrick, who fortify me with love, laughter, spice, and normalcy throughout my daily life; my high-school teachers Judy Dufford and Susan Dar, who have stayed long past graduation as deeply cherished friends; Don Barnes, who enjoyed bacon, eggs, and a naughty joke; and my dog, Lady, who patiently spent countless, lonely hours wondering when I would come back out to play. ❧

N

FREUND'S
FARM MARKET

SWEET WIND
FARM

HOUSE OF HAYES
DAIRY FARM

WINTERBROOK
FARM

BUSH MEADOW
FARM

FORT HILL
FARMS & GARDENS

JOHNNY
APPLESEED'S FARM

MILLIX
FAMILY FARM

CRANBERRY
HILL FARM

PALAZZI
ORCHARD

PUMPKIN
PAUL'S FARM

LITCHFIELD

HARTFORD

WINDHAM

TOLLAND

Hartford

FUTTNER'S
FAMILY FARM

LOCAL
FARM

BROOKSIDE
FARM II

URBAN OAKS
ORGANIC FARM

KILLAM & BASSETTE
FARMSTEAD

JOSEPH PRELI FARM
AND VINEYARD

WAYNE'S ORGANIC
GARDEN

HURRICANE
FARM

LAUREL RIDGE
GRASS FED BEEF

WALDINGFIELD
FARM

EVERGREEN
BERRY FARM

MOUNTAINTOP
MUSHROOM

MIDDLESEX

CATO CORNER
FARM

NEW LONDON

SOELTL
FARM

CEDAR MEADOW
FARM

GAZY BROTHERS
FARM

LYMAN
ORCHARDS

DEERFIELD
FARM

STARLIGHT
GARDENS

STAEHLY
FARMS

SHORTT'S FARM
& GARDEN CENTER

CECARELLI
FARM

NEW HAVEN

HOLBROOK
FARM

SPORT HILL
FARM

New Haven

New London

DAVIS
FARM

STONINGTON
SEAFOOD HARVESTERS

MILLSTONE
FARM

SHERWOOD
FARM

MID-SOUND
FISHERIES

AMBLER
FARM

TREAT
FARM

Bridgeport

FAIRFIELD

Stamford

HILLARD BLOOM
SHELLFISH

Long
Island Sound

Gardiners Bay

Napeague
Bay

Atlantic
Ocean

Houstonic River

Connecticut River

Thames River

Lake
Candlewood

0   25 Miles

0   25 Kilometers

CONTENTS

KNOW YOUR TOMATO!

As awareness of the importance of local food becomes clearer in our collective consciousness and becomes part of our everyday conversations, we still find ourselves subject to utopian nostalgia. We paint all farmers with the same brush, using one set of adjectives to describe them all, without name or identity. Our mental imagery of farming projects red barns; vast green landscapes; tidy scenes devoid of mud piles, farming equipment, half-started projects, or mostly finished chores—the kind of happy picture of silos, white farmhouses, and sweeping sunsets we see on marketing labels in the grocery store.

Farming is an art form. Highly scientific, being a farmer requires technical knowledge and an intuition of Mother Nature that we seem to have lost—or perhaps merely forgotten. There are no time clocks, no water coolers to gossip around, no sick days, no regular paycheck, and no boundaries between personal and work life. Being a farmer demands total interdependency with a multitude of issues—from sun and wind to politics and world affairs—as determining factors for a successful harvest.

I have yet to interview anyone who has the "job" of being a farmer. The farms throughout this book are tended by a wide array of individuals who are, in a sense, highly devoted artists. Should you ask, as I did, why they chose farming as a profession, you'll receive the same blank stares. Farming is a love. It is a passion.

Each of these farmers is as independently exceptional as the masters of paint and brush whose creations we hang on our walls. Connecticut's farms are a living outdoor museum. Some of their farmers invoke comfort and familiarity like Monet; others are as strange and mysterious as Dali. A few are bright and wild like Matisse, others are every bit as abstract as Pollock, and a few will draw you in with layers of hidden detail like Seurat.

Connecticut Farmer & Feast is your guide to this living museum of Connecticut farms and the people who grow our food. We hope you get a chance to meet these passionate people—these da Vincis who preserve our environment using palettes of seed and mud and sun and water.

Each farm I visited had the unique personality of the individuals who tend that plot of soil. I talked to octogenarians who fear that they're the last keepers of critical information; young, single moms who are creating farms from scratch; families who started farming to save their sick children; sixty-year-olds who can't pay the bills, have no financial security, and struggle to scrape every penny from the dirt; couples with their dream come true; and everyone else in between.

We often say "Know your farmer, know your food." Writing this book has taught me that knowing our farmers means more than name recognition at the farm market. And yes, while it may appear that a tomato at one booth is a tomato at another booth, they are *not* the same. The personalities, dreams, fears, stories, and identity of each farmer rub off on those tomatoes, on those carrots, on those beans.

Know your tomato!

And should you seek an autograph, I hope that it is also from every farmer in this book. The recipes in this book have been developed by me in my kitchen and although I created them, I have the great pleasure to name these recipes in honor of Connecticut farmers.

From their palette to your palate, meet your food and feast well.

Introduction
LOCAL FOOD MATTERS

The current marketing word du jour, "sustainable" is often associated with the sustainable agriculture movement, which had its beginnings in North America in the 1980s. This period was characterized by a wave of bank foreclosures, particularly of small and family-owned farms. Many farmers were unable to compete with the large national and international farming corporations and were forced out of business. Some in the agriculture community also blamed globalization, through international trade agreements, for the demise of many small-scale local farms.

Terry Bambrick tending tomatoes

Connecticut's farmland is disappearing at the alarming rate of roughly 8,000 acres a year. Fertile, highly productive land is being converted to residential and commercial uses at one of the fastest rates in the country. In less than twenty years, Connecticut has lost 21 percent of its farmland. If this rate of conversion continues, our remaining farmland will be gone in less than two generations.

Everyone in Connecticut reaps the benefits of farmland. From producing fresh, local food to providing pastoral vistas, farms are a vital part of our history, culture, and economy. Connecticut farms contribute $2 billion annually to our local economy, provide myriad environmental benefits, and help balance town budgets. Studies have documented that farms require less than 50 cents in town services for every dollar they generate in local taxes, while residential development costs towns more than one dollar for every dollar of revenue generated.

Local food matters. It connects people to the land. It creates opportunities for farmers to provide food directly to their customers and helps communities increase their health, build local businesses, preserve the environment, and solidify strong economic foundations for statewide growth.

Debra Tyler of Local Farm

Sustainable farming protects the environment

Defined broadly, a food system includes the foundations for food production, the social aspects of consumption, and relevant governmental and other policies, as well as the actual growing, processing, and distribution of substances that result in foods that people consume. A food system can be characterized as local, regional, national, or global. Unfortunately, a simple definition cannot capture the complexity of a food system or the social structure and mental templates that shape social activities leading to what we eat in our society.

A community food system is the part of the larger food system that is geographically located in a community or region. In the United States today, very few community food systems remain self-sufficient and independent of the larger food system. Community food systems can vary from being almost entirely self-reliant to importing all food. They may be controlled by members of a community or by outsiders.

Over the past century, misuse and overuse of chemical fertilizers and pesticides contributed heavily to the degradation of many farms and waterways throughout the United States, Canada, and other developing countries. Out of this "farm crisis" came national and international institutions and organizations of concerned citizens, producers, community organizations, businesses like the Edibles Advocate Alliance, and others. These groups all advocate for the creation of policies and laws that support new, environmentally safe approaches to producing food that will ensure the livelihood of farmers, vibrant and economically sound communities, and local living economies. A sustainable community food system is a self-reliant system that sustains people as well as the land.

A sustainable community food system, whether local or regional, is a local food web that brings food producers closer to consumers by producing fruits and vegetables or raising livestock or fish closer to the places they are sold. The closer producers are to homes and neighborhoods, the greater the access to more nutritious and affordable food and the more we are able to steward and protect our environment. A sustainable community food system supports long-term connections between farmers and consumers while meeting the economic, social, health, and environmental needs of the communities within a region.

Connecticut's food web consists of the links between farmers and growers, processors, suppliers, and local food shops, as well as other local food providers such as farmers' markets, box schemes, Community Supported Agriculture (CSA), food cooperatives, and consumers. A thriving local food web benefits Connecticut by creating new jobs and small businesses; keeping local money in the local economy; generating fewer food miles and less waste; securing thriving business models for farmers and producers; increasing access to fresh, healthy, affordable food; and expanding choices of where to shop for locally produced items and what to buy.

The future of sustainable farming in Connecticut is directly dependent on consumers and local legislation—directly dependent on *you,* both your willingness to chow down on the local bounty and to elect candidates who support local agriculture.

To preserve and grow our sustainable community food system, Connecticut must:

- Encourage local politicians to support the agricultural industry;
- Create sustainable community food systems;
- Lay the foundation of a local food distribution

system including livestock processing facilities; and
- Develop thriving local businesses and increase support for farming.

Doing so will ensure the health and vitality of our farmers and ensure scrumptious feasting around the tables of your children, their children, and their children.

How will you vote today?

Child at Sherwood Farm

Chapter 1

FAIRFIELD COUNTY

❧

AMBLER FARM

257 Hurlbutt St., Wilton, CT 06897 | (203) 834-1143 | www.amblerfarm.org

A community farm in the truest meaning of those words, Ambler Farm is owned by the town of Wilton and was purchased as an open space initiative after Betty, the last of the Amblers, died in 1998. The property is open every day of the year to all members of the community, and many come to walk their dogs, enjoy a family picnic, stop at the farm stand for organic vegetables grown on-site, or attend one of their many classes taught by volunteers, staff, or visiting farmers or experts.

Teaching gardens, stewarded by Kevin, create educational programming that has been fully integrated into the Wilton Middle School. Each year hundreds of kids become involved in this hands-on science curriculum that enhances and goes beyond their regular classroom work, enabling them to learn about botany, participate in agriculture, tend farm animals, and enjoy nature. They plant. They tend. They weed. They cultivate. They harvest. They eat.

Having always been a farm, the Ambler property has been preserved to bring out the full extent of its original character and allow the community to maintain contact with its agrarian traditions. Ambler Farm stands as a shining example of what community involvement can do to preserve open space and provide a peaceful sanctuary amidst a sea of housing and pavement.

Bring a picnic and a good book. Regardless of your age, you just might find time to hang out with resident Shetland sheep Clover and Nutmeg and their pygmy goat friends, Raymond and Betty. You can watch the baby chicks as they grow or help boil maple syrup.

Ambler Farm taps into a nostalgic remembrance of unhurried times past. There is comfort knowing that the folks at Ambler Farm are nurturing the education of our children so that they, too, will preserve more working farms for their own children's children.

I wonder if Betty thought of such grand things as she took to the front porch for tea.

3

Ambler Farm Fresh Herb Heirloom Chicken

SERVES 4

Chicken

> 1 cup kosher salt or ½ cup table salt
> ½ cup sugar
> 1 whole chicken (about 3–4 pounds)
> 2 acorn squash, halved and seeded
> 2 tablespoons butter, melted

Herb paste

> 2 tablespoons fresh thyme
> 2 tablespoons minced rosemary
> 1 tablespoon minced savory
> 1 clove garlic
> 1 teaspoon sea salt
> 2 tablespoons olive oil
> Juice of 1 lemon
> 1 whole lemon, peeled
> 1 cinnamon stick

Kids working in the Ambler Farm Gardens

1. Dissolve the salt and sugar in 2 quarts of cold water in a large container. Immerse the chicken in the brine and refrigerate for 1 hour. Preheat oven to 400°F. Remove chicken from brine, rinse thoroughly under cold running water, and dry.

2. Place chicken, breast side up, on a rack nestled into a baking dish large enough to accommodate the chicken and the squash. Surround with acorn squash halves, cut side up. Brush cut sides of squash with the melted butter.

3. Using a mortar and pestle, blend the thyme, rosemary, savory, garlic, and sea salt to a course paste. Transfer to a small bowl and blend in the olive oil and lemon juice. Gently loosen the skin on the chicken; use your fingers to rub the herb paste between the chicken meat and skin, distributing evenly across the bird. Stuff the peeled lemon and cinnamon stick into the cavity.

4. If using an heirloom chicken, roast for about 10 minutes at 400°F. Reduce heat to 325°F and continue roasting for 20 to 30 minutes longer, or until a thermometer registers 150°F on the thickest part of the breast or the cavity juices run clear when the chicken is tilted.

5. If using a conventional chicken, roast for about 10 minutes at 400°F. Reduce heat to 350°F and continue roasting for 30 to 40 minutes longer, or until a thermometer registers 160°F on the thickest part of the breast or the cavity juices run clear when the chicken is tilted.

6. Remove chicken from the oven, tent with foil, and allow to rest for at least 10 minutes. Remove the lemon and cinnamon stick from the cavity and discard. Carve and serve the chicken warm with roasted acorn squash.

Betty's Pepper Peach Salsa

SERVES 4

2 cups ripe peaches, peeled and finely diced (about 1 ½ cups)

1 cup diced red or yellow bell peppers

2 tablespoons minced red onion

4 teaspoons freshly squeezed lime juice

1 teaspoon minced chocolate mint

½ teaspoon sea salt

1 teaspoon pepper

Combine all ingredients in a medium bowl. Cover and refrigerate for at least 1 hour before serving to allow flavors to blend.

Volunteers at Ambler Farm Market Stand

HILLARD BLOOM SHELLFISH

132 WATER ST., NORWALK, CT 06854 | (203) 853-1148 | www.hillardbloomshellfish.com

Leslie Miklovich harvests Atlantic hard clams and blue-point oysters from the Connecticut side of Long Island Sound, maintaining the Hillard Bloom family operation that started in 1875. This farmer of the sea plants oysters, hunts for clams, and rotates her fields of sand in a manner consistent with the land-based concept of rotational grazing. Suction boats scoop up the clams and oysters and lift them to different beds according to water depth and temperature and nutrients, rotating their "crops" more than four times before bringing them in for harvest and to our dinner tables.

Hillard Bloom Shellfish is one of the largest clamming operations in Connecticut. Packing their shellfish in a large warehouse, and with a water farm of clam and oyster seedlings behind the building, this twelve-boat operation tends over 12,000 acres of clam and oyster beds from Greenwich to New Haven. Your favorite oysters are three years old before you can get your hands on them. Atlantic hard clams range from four to eight years old and are distinguished by size. Littlenecks are the smallest, then topnecks, then cherrystones; the largest are chowders, or quahogs. Clams have a natural lifespan of forty years, although they stop growing around the age of fifteen.

In 1947 twin brothers Hillard and Norm Bloom started this company at a time when oyster companies dominated Water Street in Norwalk. As the oyster business began to decline, the brothers started to acquire the boats and fishing beds of out-of-business fishermen who left the water for higher, drier ground. They sold chowder clams to Campbell Soup Company until the Clean Water Act of the 1970s helped Long Island Sound improve significantly enough for the farming of oysters to begin again.

Leslie Miklovich and trusty sidekick Dana Yarde are wholesalers to Boston, Philadelphia, and New York. But anyone can find their products. Just give them a

Dana Yarde and Leslie Milkovich

quick call and mosey down to the water's edge in Norwalk to pick up seafood caught that morning. With less than a fourteen-hour turnaround from sea floor to tabletop, Hillard Bloom Shellfish is a topnotch operation demanding obsessive cleanliness and near perfection in every aspect, including impeccable customer service from Dana, a paradox with her chirpy professional demeanor and her innate shyness.

Leslie and her two siblings, children of Hillard Bloom, are keeping the company in the family. Employee turnover is almost nil, with most of their employees having been around for more than twenty-five years—a huge testimony of their respect for this farming operation. Dana's husband, Jeff, who continues to captain the *Dauntless,* is more bashful than Dana, if you can believe it.

As for the future? "We're going to continue to do everything just like our father taught us," Leslie says. And they should. Hillard Bloom shellfish are prized for their creamy and crisp taste, compliments of the salinity of the waters so close to numerous freshwater rivers that flow down through Connecticut and into Long Island Sound. They continue to use a fleet of old wooden boats from the early 1900s, maintained annually on a floating dry dock in Bridgewater. Just the sight of these hand-hewn beauties chugging into port gives one the feeling of times gone past—a comforting symbol of quality and commitment, ancestral homage, and honest stewardship. All of the same feelings you get while relaxing with Leslie and Dana over coffee in the office.

Hillard Bloom's Butter Mignonette

SERVES 4

    1 tablespoon coarsely ground white or black
      peppercorns
    ½ cup white wine vinegar
    2 tablespoons finely chopped shallots
    1 teaspoon sea salt
    3 tablespoons butter, melted

1. Combine pepper, white wine vinegar, shallots, and sea salt. Whisk in melted butter.

2. Spoon onto chilled raw oysters or clams on the half shell. Devour immediately.

A clam and oyster farm

Leslie's Saffron Oyster Sauce

SERVES 4

    1 cup halved pearl onions
    ½ cup sliced asparagus stems
    2 tablespoons butter
    1 cup heavy cream (or ½ cup cream and ½ cup clam
      juice)
    1 teaspoon saffron
    3 dozen oysters, shucked and rinsed
    2 tablespoons finely chopped parsley
    Sea salt and pepper to taste
    4 thick slices county bread, toasted
    Lemon wedges

1. In a medium stockpot, sauté pearl onions and asparagus stems in butter until the onions are soft and not yet brown.

2. Add cream and saffron; simmer on low heat until the cream thickens.

3. Add the oysters and cook for about 2 more minutes on low heat until the oysters are cooked and their liquid has absorbed into the cream.

4. Add parsley, sea salt, and pepper. Serve over toasted country bread and garnish with lemon wedges.

HOLBROOK FARM

145 TURKEY PLAIN RD., BETHEL, CT 06801 | (203) 792-0561 | www.holbrookfarm.net

As the sun rises over Holbrook Farm, the day starts with the official releasing of the chickens from their nighttime quarters, freshly brewed coffee, and hot scones fresh from the oven.

Never shy of words, possessing an incredible scope of knowledge, and fizzing with a robust wit and sense of humor, John and Lynn Holbrook have cultivated their four acres free of pesticides for more than thirty years.

Land limitations, in both availability and cost, are significant obstacles unique to farming in Fairfield County. Less capacity for crop rotation is a dilemma that Farmer John has keenly overcome. He rotates the dirt. Yes, the dirt.

Holbrook Farm welcomes donations from anybody with compostables such as leaves, grass clippings, or manure to be turned into brand-new dirt. John then refortifies each row of crops, raising the dirt six inches. Five different rotations of crops are grown per row. Each row is companion planted, again five crops wide. Taking advantage of the county's current lack of composting facilities, John and Lynn have turned their four acres into a twenty-acre organic food-producing machine.

John and Lynn are feisty agropreneurs in their second careers. John, a former marketing guru, and Lynn, a high-school French teacher, have created a food lover's paradise along a busy Route 53. The flowers they companion plant to assist their vegetable production go out for weddings or perhaps, if you're lucky, right to your kitchen table.

Whatever you require, you'll find it in the cozy refurbished barn (the original Onion Barn from Westport) that serves as Holbrook Farm's farm stand: eggs, locally produced milk and cheeses, fresh bread from the oven compliments of the Lady Lynn chef du jour, organic vegetables you can't help eating before you get your seat belt on, and, according to John, the best bacon in the entire world. He recommends that you don't ever buy it—that you leave the bacon sitting nicely in their freezer. For it is of such perfection that you would be forever dissatisfied with any other bacon. "You'll be ruined," he says. Forever.

Dare ye?

Lynn Holbrook

Farmer John's Roasted Potatoes

SERVES 4

5 slices thick-cut bacon

1½ to 2 pounds of potatoes, scrubbed and cut into
1¼-inch pieces

4–6 shallots, peeled and sliced

1 tablespoon fresh thyme

1 teaspoon sea salt

1 teaspoon pepper

1. Cook bacon in a skillet over medium-high heat until crisp. Set aside. Transfer about 2 tablespoons of the remaining bacon fat to a roasting pan large enough to hold the potatoes without crowding.

2. Toss the potatoes and shallots with the fresh thyme and bacon fat in the roasting pan. Sprinkle with sea salt and pepper.

3. Roast in a 400°F oven, stirring or shaking every 15 minutes, until the potatoes are tender and evenly browned, about 45 minutes.

4. Garnish with crumbled bacon and serve.

Holbrook Farm Breakfast Scones

MAKES 9 OR 10 SCONES

2 cups all-purpose flour
1 teaspoon cream of tartar
½ teaspoon baking soda
½ teaspoon sea salt
¼ teaspoon nutmeg
¼ cup finely chopped walnuts
2 tablespoons orange zest
½ cup milk or cream
2 tablespoons maple syrup
¼ cup freshly squeezed orange juice
4 tablespoons unsalted butter, chilled and cut into
  ½-inch pieces

1. Adjust oven rack to the middle position and heat the oven to 450°F.

2. Sift all dry ingredients and spices into a large bowl. Add the walnuts and orange zest. Toss to combine.

3. In a separate bowl, combine the milk or cream, maple syrup, and orange juice.

4. With a pastry blender or two knives, cut the butter into the flour-and-nut mixture until the mixture resembles coarse meal with a few slightly larger butter lumps.

5. Make a well in the center of the flour mixture and pour in the liquid mixture. Working quickly, blend the ingredients together into a soft, slightly wet dough.

6. Turn the dough onto a well-floured work surface and quickly roll out to ½ inch thick. Using a slightly greased and floured biscuit cutter, stamp the dough, cutting close together to generate as few scraps as possible.

7. Place dough rounds 1½ inches apart on a greased baking sheet. Bake until scones are lightly brown, about 10–12 minutes. Serve immediately.

John and Lynn Holbrook

MILLSTONE FARM

180 Millstone Rd., Wilton, CT 06897 | (203) 834-2605 | www.millstonefarm.org

Betsy and Jesse Fink established Millstone Farm in 2007 to create and sustain an intimate relationship with the earth and animals. It is happily stewarded by the famous Farmer Annie, who makes it very clear that dirt under one's fingernails is quite sexy.

Farming since 2007, Betsy and Jesse wanted to grow their own food and wanted to understand the process and the requirements of such an endeavor. Epitomizing how agriculture has changed over time, Millstone Farm explores the pressures placed upon the agricultural sector and investigates how society can turn the process of growing and providing food back into the hands of a family farmer. The question is: How does each of us become productive in our own food system?

While Millstone Farm started as an intellectual endeavor, Betsy and Jesse also have found something quite personal, and unexpected. "I've come to love the sense of community that we've created here," Betsy said. "These relationships with chefs and community members are an interconnected collaboration of very different people who participate with the same food for very different reasons. Growing spinach has yielded human interconnectedness." Millstone Farm continues to be an atypical farming operation, with quantity production remaining nowhere a top priority. Instead the Finks are creating a space of balance—balance between both food and people and food and the ecosystem of their particular, fragile territory.

Farm manager Annie Farrell designed and implemented Betsy and Jesse's food-growing dreams at Millstone Farm. Her love is the garden—dirt digging is where she is the happiest—although she professes to dabble in livestock and helps tend the symbiotic relationships among land, animals, and food around the property. This organic farmer is simply brilliant. Chefs flock to Annie, both for a hug and for baskets of pristine produce. She's everybody's loving grandmother. A perfect mix of tenderness and a wily, dry humor, Annie is a renowned educator and activist who systematically demolishes the myths and misconceptions of food production.

Ever progressive, Millstone Farm continues to explore a new, twenty-first-century paradigm of food production: the blending of landholders with people who have farming skills, despite land prices that remain almost unaffordable and the shrinking of the family unit upon which family farms depend.

On a visit to Millstone Farm, you're likely to find Betsy and Jessie cradling lambs, Annie chuckling with the Chicken Man as they rotate the custom-built coops, and the phone ringing off the hook from people calling in search of food, advice, or horse-riding lessons.

Farm manager Annie Farrell with a co-worker

Betsy and Jesse Fink

Millstone Farm Tart Herb Salad

SERVES 8

> 1 clove garlic, halved lengthwise

Dressing

> 2 teaspoons freshly squeezed lemon juice
>
> 1 teaspoon sea salt
>
> 2 tablespoons extra virgin olive oil
>
> 1 teaspoon hot water

Salad

> 4 cups shredded arugula
>
> 1 cup shredded fresh spinach
>
> 2 cups shredded watercress
>
> 1½ cups shredded escarole
>
> ½ cup parsley leaves
>
> ¼ cup fresh basil leaves
>
> 10 whole sage leaves
>
> 20 fresh tarragon leaves
>
> 5 chives, diced
>
> 1 teaspoon black pepper

1. Rub the cut side of the garlic over the inside of a large salad bowl. Add the lemon juice and sea salt to the bowl.

2. Spear the garlic halves on a dinner fork. Using this as a whisk, add the olive oil and hot water to the salad bowl, whisking constantly until the dressing has an intensity of garlic that you like. Discard the garlic.

3. Add the greens and herbs and toss well. Garnish with ground pepper; toss again and serve.

Note: Just about any greens and herbs can be used. If you don't have all the ingredients, not to worry. Substitute whatever you do have!

Farmer Annie's Celery Root Remoulade

SERVES 6

> 1 medium celery root, about 1½ pounds
>
> 2 small green apples
>
> 2 tablespoons fresh lemon juice
>
> ½ cup whole-milk yogurt
>
> 1 teaspoon ground sea salt
>
> 2 teaspoons apple cider vinegar
>
> 1 tablespoon grainy Dijon mustard
>
> ½ teaspoon minced shallots
>
> 1 teaspoon honey

1. Grate the celery root and apples on a box grater or in a food processor. Immediately toss with lemon juice in a medium bowl; cover and refrigerate.

2. In a separate bowl, whisk together the yogurt, sea salt, cider vinegar, mustard, shallots, and honey. Cover and refrigerate for at least 1 hour.

3. To serve, combine celery and apples and the yogurt mixture. Serve with a liberal sprinkling of pepper.

Sal & Tom's
EASTON
HONEY
All Natural
Native Raised

CONNECTICUT
GROWN
Roma
Tomatoe $1.75

Sherwood farm

FRESH EGGS
SALAD MIX
SPINACH
BEETS
KALE
BLUEBERRIES
RADISH
BASIL   SQUASH
CUCUMBERS

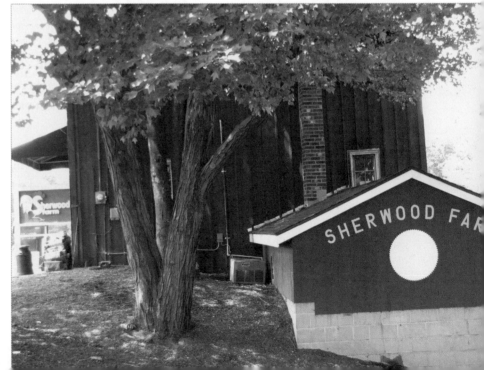

SHERWOOD FAR

Sherwood Farm

355 Sport Hill Rd., Easton, CT 06612 | (203) 268-6705 | www.sherwoodfarm.org

Tom Sherwood's farm market stand is usually bursting at the seams with food-hungry people whose arms are loaded with fresh, locally grown produce.

Tom is the sixteenth generation of Sherwoods to tend this land, and this father of two wonders about perpetuating the family name and the seventeenth generation of farming. His lovely daughters are six and eight, and while he dreams of his leading ladies going to college, he worries that he might end up in the position many of today's farmers find themselves in: sixty years old with no one around to help maintain the farm.

Sherwood Farm grows ninety different kinds of vegetables—just about anything one can think of—on ninety-two planted acres. Surrounding the farm stand are fields growing just a small sampling of everything the farm produces for quick picking when the farm stand runs short. With continuous picking throughout the day to keep up with the constant demand, this farm stand functions as a veritable grocery store on this intertown highway.

Farming seems a natural fit for Tom, who spent his childhood roaming the fields. As for having taken over the family farm, Tom gets nervous. "I always told my grandmother that I didn't want to be the one to accidentally mess it up." It's a larger responsibility than most realize—400 years of family legacy rests on Tom's shoulders.

At 3:00 a.m. this blue-eyed giant is out of bed and in the fields with flashlights to prep for CSA shares and to stock the food shed. Sherwood Farm is consciously diversified to mitigate potential crop failures. And with the knowledge that his grandmother received more money per pound of tomatoes when she was at the helm than he does today, Tom is constantly on the hunt for perfect crop rotations to keep the land profitable—regardless of the cold winter months. Every year, Tom adds and expands in new ways.

Tom Sherwood

Behind the farm stand are contented cows and chickens surrounded by towheaded children holding grass in their outstretched arms. The shrieks of children in pure wonderment as bovine heads nuzzle their fingers adds an unspoken dialogue to the story of Sherwood Farm.

Tom is the astute keeper of this family farming institution, and despite his fears that perhaps he's not working hard enough or he might make mistakes, this young man would make any grandmother proud. Because of his efforts, Sherwood Farm will continue to prosper long into the future.

Farmer Tom's Sweet Potato Casserole

SERVES 6 TO 8

7 pounds (6 to 8 medium) sweet potatoes

Filling

2 eggs
3 tablespoons extra virgin olive oil
Juice from 1 lemon
1 teaspoon sea salt
½ teaspoon ground nutmeg
½ teaspoon ground pepper
1 tablespoon vanilla extract

Streusel

2 cups whole walnuts, softened for 5 minutes in warm water
3 tablespoons maple syrup
1 teaspoon sea salt
Zest from one lemon, minced

1. Adjust the oven rack to lower-middle position and preheat oven to 400°F.

2. Poke sweet potatoes with a fork and space evenly on a rimmed baking sheet covered with foil. Bake potatoes, turning once, until they are very tender, about 40 minutes.

3. Remove potatoes from the oven and cut in half lengthwise. Allow to cool slightly before scraping out the flesh from the skins.

4. For the filling: Blend eggs, olive oil, lemon juice, vanilla extract, and spices in a food processor. Add half the sweet potatoes, and blend to desirable consistency.

5. Combine the smooth puree with the remaining potatoes. Pour filling into prepared 9 x 13-inch baking dish that has been coated with olive oil. Spread into an even layer.

6. For the streusel: Toss walnuts in maple syrup to moisten. Sprinkle the nuts with sea salt and lemon zest, and toss until evenly coated.

7. Sprinkle streusel over the filling in the baking dish. Arrange into an even layer. Cover with foil and cut a hole in the center of the foil to allow steam to escape.

8. Bake covered at 375°F for 30 minutes. Remove foil and continue baking until topping is well browned, nuts are toasted, and the filling is slightly puffy around the edges—at least another 15 minutes.

9. Allow to cool 10 minutes before serving.

Sherwood Farm Roasted Beet Salad

SERVES 4

> *1 pound beets, diced*
> *2 tablespoons olive oil*
> *1 teaspoon maple syrup*
> *1 teaspoon sea salt*
> *1 teaspoon pepper*

Salad

> *3 tablespoon balsamic vinegar, divided*
> *1 teaspoon lemon juice*
> *¼ cup coarsely chopped walnuts*
> *3 tablespoons extra virgin olive oil*
> *6 cups shredded lettuce*
> *2 ripe pears, cored and diced*
> *¼ cup crumbled goat or feta cheese*

1. Preheat oven to 375°F. Toss beets with olive oil, maple syrup, sea salt, and pepper. Roast in a casserole dish large enough to keep beets loosely separated until they're tender and starting to brown, about 30 minutes.

2. Scoop hot roasted beets into a medium-size bowl and add 2 tablespoons balsamic vinegar and the lemon juice. Stir to combine; season to taste with sea salt and pepper.

3. In a small, dry skillet, toast the walnuts until just starting to brown. Remove from heat. Spoon the walnuts into a separate bowl.

4. To the hot skillet add the 3 tablespoons of olive oil and 1 tablespoon balsamic vinegar. Stir to combine.

5. Toss salad greens with sliced pears. Add the vinaigrette and toss to combine.

6. To serve, place a mound of greens on each plate. Place beets on top and garnish with toasted walnuts and crumbled goat cheese.

Shortt's Farm & Garden Center

52 Riverside Rd., Sandy Hook, CT 06482 | (203) 426-9283 | www.shorttsfarmandgarden.com

Take a short trek down a dirt road, and shining before you like a hidden gem will be Shortt's Farm & Garden Center. This land is the original site of a dairy farm containing a river, a swamp, and grazing cattle—a common sight many years ago. Today only one dairy farm is left in the Newtown region. In the 1930s the marsh was filled in, the river diverted, and the property converted from a dairy farm to flat land hosting a sand and gravel and construction business. As a kid, Jim Shortt played on this land, riding his dirt bike and enjoying other high-flying activities both known and, probably, unknown to parental authorities.

Jim Shortt

When Jim and his mother purchased the land in 1995, they slowly began adding compost to the twelve feet of sand and gravel to create workable farmland. They sold both feed and grain for a number of years while Jim still worked in the construction business. A beautiful young lady, wedding bells, and the sad passing of Jim's mother were the beginnings of the evolution to the eight-acre growing operation that is the Shortt's Farm & Garden Center today. Shortt's is a fully certified organic operation and a member of the Connecticut Chapter of the Northeast Organic Farming Association (CT NOFA). Jim and Suzy produce the healthiest, freshest, most nutritious food possible, raised without synthetic fertilizers, pesticides, or hormones. They continue to offer custom design and construction of patios, walkways, walls, and water gardens, as well as sell produce, perennials, compost, and Fafard cedar mulch. If you want a CSA share, the early birds get the worm-healthy dirt!

Jim is a blond, wispy-haired knockout with cut-off sleeves and bulging biceps. You'll probably catch country music in the background, and he's camera shy—at first. Jim and Suzy just bought an additional piece of land with a house, barn, and ten additional certified organic growing acres. They're moving the produce operation up the hill and will reassign the current gardens to pick-your-own organic blueberry and strawberry fields. Jim is passionate about his stewardship of the land, the politics of growing food, and providing clean, wholesome, unadulterated food.

A visit to the farm stand at Shortt's Farm & Garden Center is thoroughly enjoyable, and this couple is fun to talk to. Their homemade pies, jams, jellies, and other products are worth the trip down. From agricultural land to commercial operations and back again, this farm has more than nine lives. So does Jim, no doubt.

Farmer Jim's Ground-Cherry Pie

MAKES 1 9-INCH PIE

   3 cups ground-cherries, husked
   1 recipe Farmer Erica's Perfect Piecrust (page 199) or
      2 uncooked refrigerated piecrusts
   ½ cup packed brown sugar
   2 tablespoons flour
   1 tablespoon unsalted butter
   3 tablespoons brandy (or ¼ teaspoon almond extract)
   1 teaspoon sea salt

1. Preheat oven to 425°F. Wash the ground-cherries and place in an unbaked pie shell.

2. Mix brown sugar, flour, butter, brandy, and sea salt in a bowl. Rub with fingers to evenly distribute the butter and brandy. Sprinkle over the ground-cherries.

3. Add top layer of piecrust dough, trimming the excess and sealing the edges.

4. Just before baking, reduce oven temperature to 375°F. Cut a few decorative steam vents in the dough and bake for 20 to 35 minutes, until crust has browned evenly. Turn the oven off and open the door slightly. Allow the pie to rest in the oven for about 5 to 10 more minutes. Remove from oven and place on a wire rack to cool to room temperature.

Shortt's Farm Gingered Berry Sangria

MAKES 1 LARGE PITCHER, 2–3 QUARTS

   1 cup strawberries, quartered
   1 cup blueberries
   1 cup raspberries
   1 inch fresh ginger, peeled and quartered
   1½ cups vodka
   ¼ cup packed dark brown sugar
   1 750 ml bottle red Spanish Rioja wine
   2 cups ginger ale
   Ice cubes
   Mint sprigs for garnish

1. In a large pitcher, combine strawberries, blueberries, raspberries, ginger, vodka, and brown sugar. Mix very well. Cover and refrigerate for at least 1 hour or overnight.

2. Discard the ginger and stir vigorously to make sure the brown sugar has dissolved.

3. Just before serving, stir in the wine, ginger ale, and ice cubes.

SPORT HILL FARM

596 Sport Hill Rd., Easton, CT 06612 | (203) 268-9526 | www.sporthillfarm.com

Widely known as Farm Gal, Patti Popp is really fun. In addition to her biological children, Patti is continuously followed by her forty other "babies." Her devoted chickens know a good lady when they see one.

A "self-taught farm girl who has never done this kind of work in her life," Patti decided to clear six acres of land and jumped into farming headfirst. Lo these four years later, she can finally say that she thinks she's figured it out. Despite the curveballs that Mother Nature has thrown and will continue to throw, this determined spirit has settled into a comfort zone—learning the hard way at every step. Patti blames her husband for catching her on a sleep-deprived day and mentioning that they *could* just clear the woodland on the property and create an organic garden since there was none in the vicinity. A foggy nod while sipping coffee sealed the deal.

It took six years before Sport Hill Farm started production, and Patti experienced many ups and downs along the way. The infamous Connecticut potatoes, gigantic rocks, were used to build retaining walls that now surround the farm. Her incorrect assumption that once a plant was in the ground it just continued to grow all season made her inaugural CSA year with twenty-two brave participants a challenging one. She wonders if they still like zucchini and cucumbers after having received thousands of them, and little else, that

first year. Today, having come a long way, Patti celebrates her brand-new barn.

Concentrating on teaching children, Patti and Sport Hill Farm offer a wide array of hands-on education, including planting a pizza patio garden and offering a Chicken Little class that introduces three- to five-year-olds to these feathered, egg-laying creatures.

"Farming is a wonderful thing," says this dynamic mom. "I want to keep teaching and helping kids get in touch with nature. I'm concerned with the future. Our farmers are getting older, and we need to plant the seed of passion in the younger generation. Without that, we may continue to lose farmland." Wise words from this do-it-yourself agropreneur.

For the grown-ups, Patti has both CSAs and a revolutionary new service called Crop Cash, which is a house account of prepaid credit for anything offered in the farm store—organic vegetables and eggs from Sport Hill Farm or milk, cheeses, honey, or anything else offered by neighboring farms.

Taking one day off per week, Wednesday, to do household chores and enjoy quiet time with her kids, Patti believes that she'll keep growing in knowledge, that Sport Hill Farm will keep growing, and that food from the soil will keep growing. She likes to contemplate these prospects.

And the favorite moments in this nouveau farm gal's life? Those moments in the fall when, finally, everything is in the ground and she's just waiting for the frost, thinking about the whole season and remembering the endless hours of planting seedling trays on cold, brittle March days—and looking around to see the world in full bloom and the bumper crops of the fall harvest. One picnic table has Patti's name on it. That is where she sits and enjoys her participation in the magic of growing food.

Sport Hill Farm Fresh Tomato Sauce

SERVES 6

> 1 large tomato, cut into a medium dice (peeling and seeding optional)
> 1 teaspoon maple syrup
> 1 cup whole-milk yogurt
> 3 tablespoons minced mint
> ½ teaspoon cumin
> Sea salt and pepper to taste

Mix tomatoes and maple syrup in a medium bowl. Toss to combine. Add remaining ingredients and set aside at room temperature for at least 1 hour to allow the flavors to blend.

Note: If you'd like to make this sauce ahead, keep it in the refrigerator until 1 hour before serving. You may also add 2 tablespoons chopped scallions or ¼ cup diced, seeded cucumber.

This is an exceedingly versatile sauce. Use as a dipping sauce for fresh fruits or vegetables, spoon on breads as a spread for sandwiches or on bruschetta for broiling, serve over chicken or fish, use as a light salad dressing for greens or shredded carrots, or ladle over cheeseburgers.

Patti's Crispy Saged Cauliflower and Ravioli

SERVES 4

    5 tablespoons extra virgin olive oil
    3 garlic cloves, thinly sliced
    ½ teaspoon red pepper flakes
    10 large sage leaves, sliced into strips
    2 cups cauliflower florets, cut into ½ inch pieces
    1 pound fresh cheese ravioli
    1 teaspoon sea salt
    1 teaspoon pepper
    ¼ cup freshly grated Parmesan cheese

1. In a heavy 1-quart saucepan, combine oil, garlic, and red pepper flakes. Sauté over low heat until the garlic just begins to brown. Remove from heat; scoop out the garlic and reserve.

2. Return the saucepan to low heat and add the sage leaves. Sauté until the sage begins to darken and get crispy. Remove from heat; scoop out the sage leaves and add to the garlic.

3. Bring a large pot of salted water to a boil. Add the cauliflower and boil for 3 minutes. Add the pasta and cook until al dente. (If using dried cheese ravioli, add both the cauliflower and pasta at the same time, since the cooking time will be longer.)

4. Scoop out ½ cup of the cooking water and set aside. Drain the pasta and cauliflower.

5. Add ¼ cup of the pasta water to the saucepan with the garlic and sage oil; bring to a boil. Boil vigorously for 30 seconds, stirring continuously, until an emulsified sauce forms.

6. Toss the pasta and cauliflower with the sage-oil sauce. Stir in the reserved garlic and sage leaves. Add sea salt and pepper to taste. Serve immediately with Parmesan.

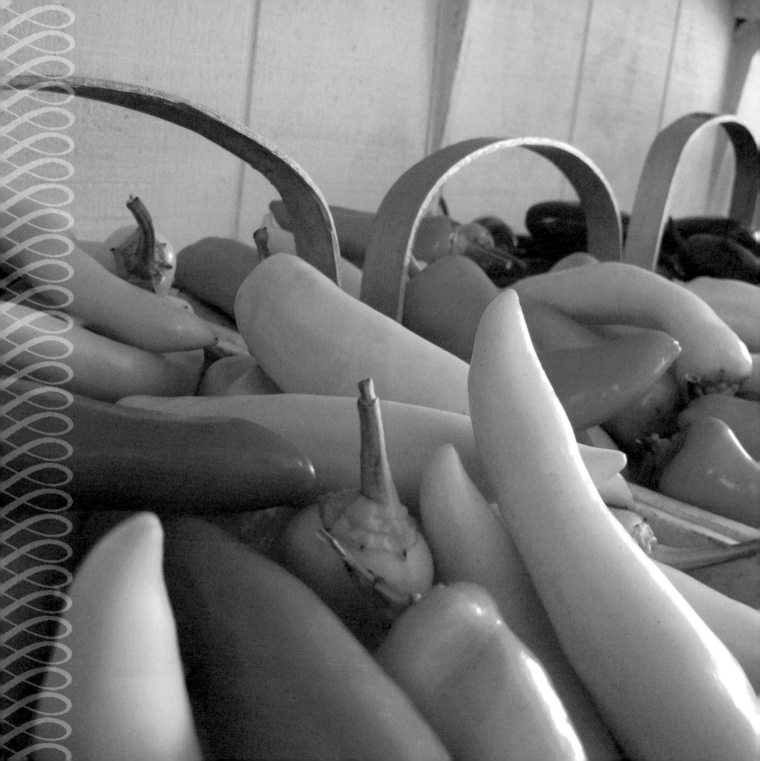

Chapter 2

HARTFORD COUNTY

❧

FUTTNER'S FAMILY FARM

910 Silver Lane, East Hartford, CT 06118 | (860) 569-4138 | www.futtnerfarm.com

Jimmy's ticker isn't what it used to be. While medical professionals demand that Jim take myriad heart-reinforcing drugs to keep him alive, his wife and best friend, Honora, believes also in the value of good, wholesome food, grown to perfection at their own Futtner's Family Farm. One or the other or both treatments have worked so far. A man who has been driving tractors since he was five, Jim hasn't experienced the electric shock paddles yet, but the emergency trips to the hospital are coming more quickly now. It's tiring.

More exhausting is the astronomical cost of health insurance that threatens to crush Jim and Honora Futtner's farming operation. Jim, who will be sixty-three, and Honora, sixty-two, are faced with a dire choice: Do they mortgage the house or go without health insurance?

"It's wrong," says Honora. "Everything we've worked for. We can't just go out and get another job that offers health insurance. This is what we love to do—we wouldn't dream of doing anything else—but farming doesn't bring in enough money to help us cover the basic health insurance costs."

Their monthly premium is $1,729.89. That is nearly $21,000 per year, plus a $5,700 annual deductible. What should they do? This conundrum keeps them awake at night—as it does many other farming families across Connecticut.

Jim and Honora Futtner

Jim and Honora requested that this part of their story be told here. They want their story to inspire politicians to understand these monumental issues that threaten the viability of Connecticut farmers and then go forth on their behalf, championing system change and health reform.

The history of Futtner's Family Farm is an interesting one. Jimmy is a third-generation farmer of Italian heritage. Tired of living in the city, and not terribly proficient in English, Jim's great-grandfather, Biase, emigrated again—this time out of dirty, urban Hartford

into the vast and wide-open countryside of East Hartford, taking a job at the Silver Lane Pickle Factory.

A reminder of the value of preserving farmland, Jim and Honora's farm stand is now squashed between commercial businesses on a busy five-lane commuter road. Just a few years ago, the Futtners sold farming acreage across the street. Now the farmland is gone. In its place stand a slew of ticky-tacky houses—all white, all identical, all for sale.

When the pickle factory was sold to Heinz, Jim's grandfather created Futtner's Family Farm, which specialized in commercial crops with well over 120 acres of carrots and cabbage. This grand-scale commercial operation sold these two products to the US Army, Air Force, Navy, and Marines. Until 1972 they sold to canneries in Delaware. When Jim tired of the carrot business, the Futtner's Family Farm Market Stand was born, selling diversified crops to retail consumers. Today they grow flowers, plants, and vegetables in 2,500 square feet of greenhouses.

In less than five minutes, you can tell that Jimmy and Honora are still deeply in love with each other. Deep interdependence and friendship emanate from them—sometimes in the way they forget to talk out loud because each already knows what the other is going to say. I asked if they had had a torrid, whirlwind romance.

With a gleam, Jimmy whispered, "Well, once we got going, it was pretty good! After thirty-seven years, the time has flown by too quickly." As for Honora, "I'd like him around for a while. He's just really nice."

Their children all remain in the East Hartford area today. It isn't uncommon to see the entire Futtner clan gathered together for an impromptu lunch around the picnic table out back.

Farmer Jimmy's Watermelon Gazpacho
SERVES 4

    3 cups seedless watermelon puree
    1 cup diced, seeded watermelon
    1 cup diced, seeded tomato
    1 cup peeled, seeded cucumbers, diced small
    ½ cup diced red pepper
    3 tablespoons lime juice
    ¼ cup minced cilantro leaves
    1 teaspoon minced fresh ginger
    ½ small jalapeño, seeded and minced (optional)
    3 tablespoons minced green onion
    Sea salt and pepper to taste

1. Puree large cubes of watermelon in a blender until smooth. Measure 3 cups.

2. Combine all ingredients in a large bowl. Chill in the refrigerator for at least 20 minutes.

3. Ladle into chilled soup bowls, and serve very cold.

Futtner's Family Farm Warm Cauliflower Salad
SERVES 4

    1 teaspoon Dijon mustard
    1 tablespoon apple cider vinegar
    1 tablespoon freshly squeezed orange juice
    2 teaspoons orange zest
    1 scallion, sliced thinly
    2 tablespoons fresh dill, minced
    2 tablespoons extra virgin olive oil
    1 medium head cauliflower, trimmed, cored, and cut
       into florets
    Sea salt and pepper to taste
    ½ cup toasted walnuts

1. In a small bowl, combine the mustard, vinegar, orange juice, zest, scallion, dill, and olive oil.

2. Fit a large 4-quart saucepan with a steamer basket. Pour 2 inches of water into the saucepan and bring to a boil.

3. Add cauliflower florets to basket and reduce heat to medium. Cover pan and steam until cauliflower is just tender, 5 to 7 minutes.

4. Remove cauliflower to a serving bowl; toss with the vinaigrette. Season to taste with sea salt and pepper and sprinkle with walnuts. Serve warm or cold.

HOUSE OF HAYES DAIRY FARM

151 East St., North Granby, CT 06035 | (860) 653-4157 | www.sweetpeacheese.com

Have I got a couple of taste treats for you! First, if you haven't tasted SweetPea Cheese Goat Cheese Curds, you're missing out on an experience of a lifetime. And second, you have absolutely no clue what you're missing if you haven't rolled SweetPea Cheese Greek-style goat's-milk yogurt across the roof of your mouth. Seriously.

Stanley and Dorothy Hayes operate the 250-acre House of Hayes Dairy Farm with their two children, Ellen and Daniel. (We have Dorothy and Daniel to thank for creating the SweetPea cheeses sold at the year-round farm stand, which is guarded by an overly defensive goose.) They turn milk from their herds of sixty cows and sixty-eight goats into a wide range of yogurt and chèvre and feta cheeses, using low-temperature pasteurization to ensure maximum product nutrition.

Milk sold in grocery stores is ultrapasteurized to a temperature of 280°F, a process that denatures milk protein, enzymes, vitamins, and minerals, enabling the milk to be shipped over great distances without spoiling. It has been reported that ultrapasteurized milk loses up to 66 percent of vitamins A, D, and E and 50 percent of vitamin C. This ultrapasteurized milk cannot be turned into cheese or whipped into cream without the addition of chemical stabilizers.

Ultrapasteurized milk tastes flat and watery compared to the options available from local farmers.

Stanley and Dorothy slowly heat their milk to 150°F for thirty minutes, which accounts for both the elite flavor of their products and their increased nutritional value. You don't need to fortify House of Hayes's milk or dairy products with calcium or vitamin D. They didn't destroy these nutrients in the first place.

The Hayes family has farmed this land for fourteen generations, and over the years the farm has changed names from Brookside Farm to House of Hayes Dairy. Stanley continues to grow and diversify the agricultural operation. He might build a cheese cave from a series of crumbling brick buildings remaining on the property

Stanley Hayes

Sweet Pea Cheese

"Enriching and Sustaining Agriculture in the Town of Granby."

Whole Cow
Milk Yogurt

Sell By: 8-31
The Hayes Family
151 East St. N. Granby, CT
860-653-4157
www.sweetpeacheese.com
Ingredients: Whole cow's milk, Cultures

CHEESE
SHOP
OPEN
DAILY

from the 1930s and 1940s. This would enable Hayes House of Dairy to expand into hard cheeses such as Cheddar, Gouda, and Parmigiana Reggiano or ripened cheeses such as blue, Camembert, and Brie. The sky is the limit for the Hayes family and their farm.

Asked if, of all of the professions he could have chosen, he still would be a farmer, Stanley just throws his hands out to the side and says, "I grew up here!" Pretty stupid question in the first place.

House of Hayes Spicy Peaches

SERVES 4

> 2 pounds peaches, ripe but still firm
> ¾ cup maple syrup
> 1 cinnamon stick
> 1 teaspoon allspice
> 1 teaspoon whole cloves
> 2 tablespoons thinly sliced fresh ginger
> 2 cups dry white wine

1. Peel and quarter peaches.

2. Combine remaining ingredients in a 4-quart nonreactive pot, and simmer until reduced by half.

3. Remove from heat. Add peaches and allow to cool to room temperature.

4. Serve as a dessert with freshly made Stanley's Cinnamon Yogurt Ice Cream (recipe follows) or as an accompaniment to baked ham.

Stanley's Cinnamon Yogurt Ice Cream

SERVES 4

> 2 cups heavy cream
> 1 teaspoon ground cinnamon
> ½ cup maple syrup
> 6 large egg yolks
> 1 teaspoon sea salt
> 2 cups Greek-style goat's-milk yogurt (or cow's-milk yogurt), at room temperature

1. Combine the cream, cinnamon, and maple syrup in a heavy 4-quart saucepan. Cook, stirring frequently, over medium heat until almost simmering.

2. In a bowl, whisk together the egg yolks and sea salt. Add the yogurt, and whisk to combine.

3. Slowly pour 1 cup of the hot cream liquid into the egg-and-yogurt mixture, whisking as you pour.

4. Return the warmed mixture to the saucepan. Cook over low heat, stirring constantly with a spatula, until the custard reaches 175°F on a candy thermometer and lightly coats the back of the spatula.

5. Remove the custard from heat and cool to room temperature in an ice bath. Refrigerate the custard until cold, about 1 to 2 hours.

6. Churn custard in an ice-cream machine according to the manufacturer's instructions. Freeze until scoopable, about 4 hours, depending on your machine.

7. Serve with House of Hayes Spicy Peaches, fresh summer fruit, Palazzi Orchard Apple Pumpkin Pie (page 202), or all by itself with a dash of brandy.

Joseph Preli Farm and Vineyard

235 Hopewell Rd., South Glastonbury, CT 06073 | (860) 633-7333

John Yushkevich has come back home. This grandson of Joseph Preli, who purchased this farm in 1920, has rebuilt areas of the family homestead to include a workable family farm. The Concord grapes on the farm predate his grandfather's purchase, making them more than 110 years old. Under John's guidance, the Joseph Preli Farm now boasts a wide variety of exotic and ethnic produce not found in standard markets.

Joseph and Rose Preli

Families residing throughout the Matson Hill area of South Glastonbury are descendants of immigrants from the same province of Italy and a tiny cluster of villages called Ferrara. Joseph Preli, his pregnant wife, Rose, and their two-year-old toddler walked through Ellis Island in 1910 and slowly made their way to South Glastonbury upon hearing that this part of Connecticut had terrain similar to their native homeland. So harrowing was Rose's first crossing of the Atlantic, with morning sickness and a robust two-year-old—crowded together with other families belowdecks as steerage passengers—that John's grandmother never again traveled back to her native Italy.

Crossing the Atlantic by steamship took eight to twelve days. Steerage passengers were given a burlap mattress stuffed with hay or seaweed, a life preserver that doubled as a pillow, and a tin pail and utensils for meals, which were served from a gigantic vat. Bunks in steerage were stacked two high and two wide in open compartments containing 400 to 800 passengers in the lowest area of the ship, next to the coal-fired engines and boilers. Steerage was exceedingly hot with coal dust, engine burn, and no outside airflow. No wonder Rose never wanted to board another steamship.

Between 1880 and 1920, nearly four million Italians immigrated to the United States. Their influence on Connecticut agriculture is profound, and their contributions are especially noticeable throughout Hartford County. The Preli family was among the 51 percent of families who survived the exceedingly difficult transition into the fabric of American culture; the rest returned to Italy.

John Yushkevich has been producing food at the Joseph Preli Farm and Vineyard for four years. It isn't difficult to see how happy he is. There is an air of *King of the Hill* at the tented farm stand with lawn chairs full of friends discussing the neighborhood. Still using Joseph Preli's tractors from the 1930s and 1940s, John grows his family's Italian heirloom tomatoes, peppers, eggplant, tomatillos, basil, and more. This heating, ventilating, and air-conditioning (HVAC) repairman has dreams of eventually farming and producing food full-time.

Joseph Preli
Est. 1920
Farm & Vineyard

John Yushkevich

OPEN

FRESH PEACHES

Preli Sweet Pepper Black Beans

SERVES 6

½ pound bacon, cut into ½-inch strips

Beans

1 pound dried black beans, picked over and rinsed

12 cups water

1 smoked ham hock, rinsed

2 red bell peppers, stemmed, seeded, and quartered

1 medium onion, minced

4 garlic cloves, sliced

2 bay leaves

2 teaspoons sea salt

Sofrito

2 tablespoons bacon fat

1 medium onion, minced

1 red bell pepper, minced

¼ cup fresh oregano leaves

1½ teaspoons ground cumin (preferably freshly ground seeds)

2 tablespoons balsamic vinegar (for garnish)

Sea salt and pepper to taste

1. In a 10-inch skillet over medium heat, cook bacon until crisp and brown. Transfer to a paper towel–lined plate; set aside. Reserve the skillet and bacon fat for later.

2. Bring all bean ingredients to a boil over medium-high heat in a heavy soup kettle, skimming the surface as scum rises.

3. Reduce heat to low and simmer, partially covered, until the beans are tender but not splitting, about 2 hours. Add more water if cooking liquid reduces to the level of the beans.

4. Remove the ham hock from the beans. When cool enough to handle, remove meat from the bone and cut into bite-size pieces. Set aside. Discard bone and skin.

5. To make the sofrito, heat bacon fat in a large skillet over medium heat. Add all remaining ingredients except the cumin and balsamic vinegar. Sauté until the vegetables soften, about 8 to 10 minutes. Add the cumin and sauté until fragrant, about 1 minute longer.

6. Scoop 1 cup beans and 2 cups cooking liquid into the pan with the sofrito. Mash the beans with a potato masher until smooth. Simmer over medium heat until the liquid is reduced and thickened, about 6 minutes.

7. Return sofrito mixture to bean pot. Simmer until beans are creamy and the liquid thickens to sauce consistency, about 15 to 20 minutes.

8. Add balsamic vinegar and salt and pepper to taste.

9. Serve over rice or in burritos. Add extra liquid and puree for a creamy black bean soup.

Rose's Plum Goulash

SERVES 4

3 pounds beef chuck roast, cut into 1½-inch cubes
Sea salt and ground pepper
3 tablespoons grape seed oil or lard
3 medium onions, chopped coarse
2 tablespoons grated fresh ginger
6 cups quartered fresh plums
1 tablespoon cinnamon
½ teaspoon nutmeg
½ teaspoon allspice
3 tablespoons fresh thyme
¼ cup all-purpose flour
3 cups low-sodium chicken broth
½ cup whole-milk yogurt
2 teaspoons freshly squeezed lemon juice
¼ cup fresh parsley, minced
1 pound egg noodles, cooked according to package
  directions and drained

1. Heat oven to 300°F. Dry the beef thoroughly with paper towels and season generously with sea salt and pepper.

2. Heat 1 tablespoon of the oil in a 13-quart ovenproof Dutch oven over medium-high heat. Add half the meat to the pot so that the beef pieces are not touching. Cook, not moving the beef, until the pieces are well browned, about 3 minutes. Turn each piece of beef and continue cooking until most sides are well browned, about 5 minutes longer.

Transfer the beef to a medium bowl. Add another tablespoon of oil to the pot, and repeat.

3. Reduce heat to medium, add the last tablespoon of oil and sauté the onions, stirring vigorously to loosen the browned bits, until the onions have softened and browned, about 8 minutes. Add the ginger and plums; sauté until fragrant, about 30 seconds. Add the spices, fresh thyme, and flour, and stir until the onions and plums are evenly coated, about 2 more minutes.

4. Stir in 1½ cups of the chicken broth, scraping the bottom and edges of the pan to loosen the remaining browned bits. Continue stirring until the flour is dissolved and the liquid has thickened. Gradually add the remaining broth.

5. Add the browned beef and accumulated juices. Stir to blend, submerging the beef under the liquid. Bring to a simmer, then cover the pot and place it in the oven. Cook for about 2 hours, until the meat is tender.

6. Place the yogurt and lemon juice in a medium bowl and stir about ½ cup of the hot stewing liquid into it. Stir the warmed yogurt mixture back into the stew. Stir in the parsley, and season to taste with sea salt and pepper.

7. Serve over cooked and buttered egg noodles.

*The Killam & Bassette
Farmstead is a family operation*

Killam&Bassette
So.Glastonbury
CT
Farmstead
860 633-1067

Henry Bassette

Killam & Bassette Farmstead

14 Tryon St., South Glastonbury, CT 06073 | (860) 633-1067 | www.kandbfarmstead.com

Bright tie-dyed neon-hued farm shirts announce the arrival of the proprietors of the Killam & Bassette Farmstead, an eighty-five-acre farm nestled along the Connecticut River.

The land was originally a dairy and tobacco farm, and Chris and Kevin Bassette have maintained thirteen acres of broadleaf tobacco cultivation, but they have expanded to include eggs from free-range chickens, fruits and vegetables, and jams and jellies made from the produce on their farm. Fearless in the kitchen, Chris has mastered garlic jam as well as pear-blueberry, pumpkin pie, caramel apple, and chocolate raspberry confitures. In addition to the traditional jam and jelly varieties, Chris allows for the annual creation of a few out-of-the-box preserves that are both perfect straight from the jar and extremely pleasurable to cook with.

Chris got her first job at the age of nine picking blueberries at an apple orchard. She had fallen in love for the first time, and the only way she was able to see her beau, Kevin, was to join him down in the fields. Now married, the Bassettes have chosen farming as a way of life. "Where else can you get a job where your kids can come to work with you every day?" Chris asks. "I couldn't imagine raising our kids any other way but side by side with us."

Jaime (six), Henry (nine), Dina (ten), Olivia (twelve), and Abby (fourteen) all participate in different aspects of the farm. The gregarious Jaime plays with the chickens, helps Daddy as he picks and sorts the vegetables, keeps him company as they deliver chickens to the Middlesex auction house, and goes with him to the Hartford Regional Market at 3:30 in the morning. Watching Jaime running and playing through the tobacco pickers after she's checked for eggs and observing Henry as he learns to drive a tractor 10,000 times his own weight, I can't help but think that, given the choice, most kids would rather play in the dirt than with a video game.

Jaime Bassette

Kevin has worked for Henry Killam on his farms for most of his life. As Henry grew older he partnered with the Bassettes to maintain his farm—thus creating the Killam & Bassette Farmstead. A bachelor, Henry lives happily with Chris and Kevin and has assumed the role of grandfather to their kids. You'll still find Henry out in the fields every day with Kevin and his two brothers, Dave and Scott, and nephew, Michael.

These two families have combined to create one family and one farm. Chris smiles with the hope that both the Killam & Bassette farm and family will continue to grow and prosper. "Like any farmer," she says, "I'd hate to see the land developed for housing should any one of our children not be interested in taking over the farm. But then again, with the lack of a 401(k) plan, this is very risky business."

Henry Killam, Chris & Kevin Bassette

Chris and Kevin are already planning for a bed-and-breakfast on-site when the kids are older. With siblings, aunts, uncles, and friends all stopping in to lend a hand, there is no sign the Killam & Bassette family dynasty will fade anytime soon.

Killam & Bassette Glazed Radishes

SERVES 4

  2 dozen young radishes
  ½ cup low-sodium chicken stock
  ½ cup dry white wine
  2 tablespoons butter, melted
  2 teaspoons honey
  2 teaspoons fresh chives, minced
  Sea salt and pepper

1. Cut the tops and bottoms off the radishes.

2. In a small bowl, combine chicken stock, wine, butter, and honey. Put the radishes in a sauté pan just large enough to hold them in a single layer; and pour over enough liquid, about 1 cup, to come halfway up the sides of the radishes.

3. Bring to a simmer over high heat. Turn the heat to low and simmer, turning occasionally, for about 15 minutes, or until the radishes can be poked through with a paring knife. If liquid remains, increase the heat, stirring the radishes constantly to evaporate the liquid and create a caramelized honey sauce that browns the radishes on all sides.

4. Sprinkle with chives and sea salt and pepper to taste. Serve warm.

Henry Killam's Corn Chowder

SERVES 6

10 medium ears fresh corn, husked
3 ounces salt pork cut into 2-inch cubes
1 tablespoon unsalted butter
1 large sweet onion, diced
3 tablespoons all-purpose flour
4 cups low-sodium chicken stock
2 medium red potatoes, scrubbed and cut into
   ¼-inch dice, about 3 cups
1 bay leaf
2 teaspoons fresh thyme leaves
1 large orange, peeled, sectioned, and diced
1 cup whole milk
1 cup heavy cream
Sea salt and pepper

1. Standing the corn on end, cut the kernels from 4 ears of corn. Set aside. Grate the remaining 6 ears of corn on a box grater, scraping any remaining pulp from the cobs with a butter knife. Transfer the grated corn and pulp to a second bowl and set aside.

2. Sauté the salt pork in a large stockpot over medium-high heat, pressing down on the pieces to render the fat, until the cubes are crisp and golden brown, about 10 minutes.

3. Reduce the heat to low; stir in the butter and onion, and cook until the onion has softened. Remove salt pork and set aside.

4. Stir in the flour and cook, stirring constantly, until the flour begins to brown. Whisking constantly, gradually add the stock. Add the potatoes, bay leaf, thyme, orange pieces, milk, grated corn and pulp, and reserved salt pork; bring to a boil. Reduce heat to medium-low and simmer until the potatoes are almost tender, about 8 minutes.

5. Add the reserved corn kernels and heavy cream and return to a simmer, cooking until the corn kernels are tender but slightly crunchy, about 5 minutes.

6. Discard the bay leaf and salt pork. Season to taste with sea salt and pepper. Serve warm.

Sweet Wind Farm

339 South Rd., East Hartland, CT 06027 | (860) 653-2038 | www.sweetwindfarm.net

Keeping up with Arlow Case requires a significant amount of stamina. He writes his annual maple syrup records on the bathroom wall in the sugarhouse—hand-built from wood harvested on Sweet Wind Farm—which also serves as their farm market stand, a teaching classroom, and the site where the Case family offers pancake breakfasts to hungry travelers. Bathrooms make the best offices.

Arlow Case Jr. and his wife, Susan, purchased Sweet Wind Farm with hard-earned sweat equity. They'll eventually absorb the family farm just over the border in Lanford, Massachusetts, but in the meantime, Arlow describes Sweet Wind Farm as a full-service maple farm using cutting-edge equipment and technology. He's been a maple sugar maestro since he was fourteen, when he started his first commercial business, Arlow's Sugar Shack, which sold the sweet elixir in recycled Maxwell House coffee jars for 50 cents. He certainly redefines "good to the last drop."

Arlow has built a sugarhouse like none you've ever seen before. With an 800-gallon sap storage room, miles of maple-moving tubes and pipes running along all three stories, hundreds of tanks that can hold 1,000 gallons of raw sap, pumps, and specially invented, should-be-patented filters, this sugarhouse processes more than 50,000 gallons of maple sap. With a rough conversion rate of 40 to 1, 50,000 gallons of maple sap will create about 1,000 gallons of pure maple syrup.

Unlike most syrup producers, Arlow does not vent the steam from boiling sap out through the roof. He billows the steam throughout the building, creating a maple steam bath. Contrary to popular belief, maple steam doesn't hurt the wood at all, actually preserving it. According to Arlow's uncle, the only reason you want an outdoor steam vent is so that you can see inside the building while you're working.

Arlow and Susan Case

I wondered if taking a maple steam bath would preserve youthful looks the same way it preserves wood. Susan thinks so. Everyone knows exactly where to find her in the months of February and March while Arlow is working. As for opening their doors to the public for this nearly edible beauty treatment? They're seriously thinking about it.

In addition to maple syrup, Sweet Wind Farm offers pick-your-own blueberries, tomatoes, squash, cucumbers, beans, peppers, flowers, and more. Susan spins delectable maple confections such as sugar, candy, lollipops, and jelly and oversees community programming, including cooking classes, maple and pumpkin festivals, hosted birthday parties, and sugaring classes and tours. Farming since they've known each other, this agricultural couple has come a long way from their first farm stand—a rusting card table by the side of the road.

Visiting Sweet Wind Farm, you'll no doubt find Arlow flitting around with an ear-to-ear grin. Spending time with him is really fun.

Arlow's Beer Maple Glaze

MAKES 2 CUPS OR ENOUGH FOR 6–12 POUNDS OF MEAT OR POULTRY

3 tablespoons butter
¼ cup minced shallots
2 cups Guinness or other stout
2 cups chicken stock
½ cup real maple syrup
2 tablespoons peppercorns
1 tablespoon whole cloves
⅛ teaspoon allspice
1 bay leaf
1½ tablespoons balsamic vinegar
Sea salt and pepper to taste

1. In a 4-quart saucepan, melt the butter and sauté shallots until just beginning to brown.

2. Add beer, stock, maple syrup, and spices. Simmer on low heat until reduced by half.

3. Strain and throw the spices away. Add balsamic vinegar and salt and pepper to taste, and store in the refrigerator.

4. Brush onto pork, chicken, beef, or ham before and during cooking.

Sweet Wind Farm Swiss Chard with Caper Butter

SERVES 4

4 tablespoons butter, divided

3 garlic cloves, minced

1 pound Swiss chard, washed, stems cut into ¼-inch dice and leaves into ½-inch-wide strips

2 teaspoons maple syrup

1 tablespoon capers

3 tablespoons freshly squeezed orange juice

Sea salt and pepper to taste

1. Melt 2 tablespoons of butter in a large skillet over medium heat and sauté the garlic until slightly browned.

2. Add the Swiss chard stems and sauté until tender, about 5 minutes. Add the leaves and sauté until completely limp, an additional 2 to 4 minutes. Remove to a serving bowl.

3. To the hot skillet, add the remaining 2 tablespoons of butter, maple syrup, and capers. Stir to scrape up the browned bits of garlic in the pan and to allow the capers to infuse their flavor into the butter.

4. Stir in the orange juice and pour over the Swiss chard. Season to taste with salt and pepper. Serve warm.

Maple sugaring runs in Arlow's family

organic
Jersey White Yams

$2.75/lb

Urban Oaks Organic Farm

225 Oak St., New Britain, CT 06051 | (860) 223-6200 | www.urbanoaks.org

Mike Kandefer and Tony Norris came upon the old Sandelli horticultural and floral business by accident. The property, which had been vacant for twelve years, was covered by enormous greenhouses with smashed windows and littered with 350 tractor-trailer truckloads of garbage. With a few generous grants, thousands of hours of hard labor, and a gigantic nod from the EPA, which swept in from Boston with both money and overwhelming praise for such an extensive cleanup project, Mike and Tony created Urban Oaks Organic Farm in the center of New Britain, Connecticut. In 1999 these two visionary farmers opened this nonprofit farm, which fills a few city blocks in a densely populated neighborhood of apartments, bodegas, and liquor stores.

The current site of the year-round farm market stand was once an old gas station and auto repair operation. Cleanup entailed digging twenty feet deep to remove thousands of tons of contaminated soil, transforming the place from a brownfield site to a green urban organic farm.

It was Tony who pushed forward the idea of reengineering this dilapidated property. "I first said no!" Mike laughs. "This place was such a mess. I said no way because I knew who'd be doing most of the physical work, because Tony was the numbers guy and office manager." Fortunately Tony had a winning power of persuasion—it didn't take much more than an hour for Mike to concede—and the two embarked on transforming the biggest eyesore they had ever seen.

Today Urban Oaks Organic Farm is the largest urban farm in the country, specializing in heirloom organic crops in its five greenhouses and on its four acres of tillable land. Whimsically, the greenhouses are partially crowded with colossal fig and grapefruit trees and four-foot-tall rosemary bushes. Urban Oaks offers both summer and winter CSA shares, and with a Wholesome Wave Foundation grant to double-stamp both federal Women, Infants, and Children (WIC)

program and food stamps, each food dollar goes farther in this low-income inner-city community.

Now supported by a strong and dedicated board of directors, who are required to work in the mud, Urban Oaks provides education for city residents and school groups in organic gardening methods, sustainable agriculture, nontoxic farming techniques, and composting. As the soil continues to be cleaned and improved, this education will extend into community garden plots.

Mike continues to experiment with new growing techniques and crops, adding a zesty flavor to typical vegetable gardening.

Since Tony's death in 2007, Mike continues to nurture their shared vision while pioneering a living example of a metropolitan agricultural sanctuary. A swift kick from board member Linda Glick prods Mike to take a day off every now and again. He might, but I doubt it.

Urban Oaks Orange Spaghetti Sauce

SERVES 4

> 2 teaspoons sea salt
> 1 clove garlic
> 1 teaspoon thyme
> 1 teaspoon oregano
> 1 teaspoon diced rosemary leaves
> 3 tablespoons extra virgin olive oil
> 1 yellow onion, diced
> 5 ripe tomatoes, diced
> 1 cup diced dried apricots
> 2 oranges, juiced
> Sea salt and pepper to taste

1. Combine salt, garlic, and herbs in a mortar and pestle and mash until a smooth paste forms.

2. Heat the olive oil in a skillet and sauté the onions until brown. Add the tomatoes, diced to retain their seeds and skins, the spice-and-garlic paste, and dried fruit.

3. Simmer over low to medium heat until the tomatoes release their juices and the sauce has thickened.

4. Add fresh orange juice and continue to evaporate the liquid, stirring occasionally, until reduced by half, about 10 minutes.

5. Season with salt and pepper to taste.

Mike & Tony's Winter Day Rice

SERVES 4

> 1 13.5-ounce can coconut milk
> 1 cup long grain rice
> ½ teaspoon sea salt
> ½ teaspoon pepper
> ½ teaspoon minced fresh ginger
> 1 tablespoon minced pineapple sage
> 2 tablespoons mirin (sweet Japanese rice wine)
> Sea salt and pepper to taste

Mike Kandefer

1. In a 1-quart pan add enough water to the coconut milk to yield 2¼ cups total. Bring to a boil over medium-high heat.

2. Add the long grain rice, herbs, and spices. Reduce heat and cover. Simmer on low until rice is cooked, about 10 minutes.

3. Add mirin and season to taste with salt and pepper. Serve immediately.

Note: Double-check the instructions on your rice package for the correct water-to-rice ratio, and adjust the recipe accordingly.

Chapter 3

LITCHFIELD COUNTY

BROOKSIDE FARM II

79 East Chestnut Hill Rd., Litchfield, CT 06759 | (860) 567-3890

J. Mark Harran is an avid tractor collector. He's seventy now and, as he says, "hoping for seventy-one." While his collection is not as large as it once was, you can tell that Mark worships at the throne of John Deere. Surrounded by green machines, he and his wife, Kay Carroll, operate Brookside Farm II, a notable and quite successful maple syrup operation in Litchfield.

Mark is part of a demonstration project to show that Connecticut has the potential to dramatically increase its maple syrup and maple products production and sales to more than $20 million in ten years through tapping more trees, employing technology to existing infrastructure, and modifying the marketing model of Connecticut's maple syrup industry.

Connecticut currently taps one-tenth of 1 percent of all maple trees in Connecticut for maple syrup (as a reference point, Quebec taps 33 percent of its trees). Mark believes that this state could dramatically increase its maple crop value, resulting in increased economic benefits for Nutmeggers.

Mark's father, John Allen, died at the age of fifty-nine from pancreatic cancer. This sudden and untimely loss had a profound impact on Mark, who realized that in retiring early, he might have a chance to play a bit, to enjoy the good life—something his father did not have the opportunity to do. "I haven't slowed down yet with the good life," he says. "I'm still busier than a cow tongue on a salt lick."

Among a million other things, Mark continues to work closely with Wamogo High School in Litchfield, where he is chairman of the Ag-science Advisory Council. The acting president of the Maple Syrup Producers Association of Connecticut, this seasoned veteran of the food industry is now approaching food from the ground up.

Retiring early after thirty years in service to Kraft Foods as a senior vice president of sales and marketing in Chicago, he promptly went south to the warmer winds of Florida. In 1999, at the age of sixty, and after five years swooning in the sun, Mark remembered maple sugaring days with his grandfather in Hopkinton, New York. As a kid, he would ride with his grandfather, who tapped more than 5,000 trees with a crew of six men and three teams of horses, traversing hundreds of acres seven days a week. That indelible memory from the age of four prompted him to return to Connecticut and start cultivating his own sugarbush.

His maple life has come a long way from wooden buckets and backyard, smoke-filled sugarhouses. With Mark at the helm, this agricultural commodity could very well lead Connecticut to become a powerhouse in self-sustaining food production.

J. Mark Harran

Mark is definitely unconventional, completely at home in his Carhartts and conductor's cap, yet with an intellect that would stun even the most educated. I wonder if he still plays with his 1920's-era toy tractors, displayed proudly on the library shelves. Perhaps he just limits his playtime to the real tractors in his restored 1820s barn. With a giggling gaggle of grandchildren, he will, I'm sure, pass down his love for both tractors and maple syrup to another generation.

Farmer Mark's Ricotta Pancakes

SERVES 4

3 eggs
2 cups ricotta cheese, drained in a strainer overnight
1 teaspoon sea salt
1 teaspoon cinnamon
½ teaspoon nutmeg
2 cups flour
Maple syrup

1. Whisk eggs in a large bowl. Add ricotta cheese, salt, cinnamon, and nutmeg. Stir to combine.

2. Slowly begin adding flour, stirring continuously, until a thick paste forms.

3. Heat a slightly buttered griddle or frying pan over low to medium heat. Add ricotta pancake batter one spoonful at a time, mashing the batter flat with a spatula and flipping immediately when the batter has set enough on the bottom to hold together.

4. Brown the top side of the pancake, about 1 minute. Flip the pancake again, cooking for another 30 seconds. (These pancakes cook very quickly.) Douse with maple syrup and serve warm.

Brookside Farm Maple Baked Pumpkin

SERVES 4

2 small sweet pumpkins (about 1 pound each), halved
*   from top to bottom and seeded*
¼ cup butter
1 cup minced dried prunes
4 teaspoons maple syrup
1 teaspoon grated fresh ginger
4 tablespoons heavy cream
1 teaspoon sea salt
1 teaspoon pepper

1. Preheat oven to 400°F. Arrange the pumpkin halves, flesh side up, in a square baking pan just large enough to hold the pumpkin upright. Add about ½ inch water to the bottom of the roasting pan to prevent the pumpkin from burning.

2. To the center of each pumpkin half add 1 tablespoon butter, ¼ cup minced dried prunes, 1 teaspoon maple syrup, ¼ teaspoon freshly grated ginger, 1 tablespoon heavy cream (optional), ¼ teaspoon sea salt, and ¼ teaspoon pepper.

3. Bake for 1 to 1½ hours, or until the squash feels soft when poked with a fork. Serve warm.

Zeke, the saker falcon

Bob and Cathee Alex

Evergreen Berry Farm

435 Bassett Rd., Watertown, CT 06795 | (860) 274-0825 | www.evergreenberryfarm.com

Zeke, a saker falcon, is the sleek guardian of an eleven-acre organic fruit farm. This hybrid raptor flies the skies every day with his friend and partner, falconer Bob Alex.

Connecticut is one of the last states in the Union to legalize falconry and enforces rigorous standards, including state examinations, extensive permits, more than three years of training with a master falconer, exhaustive recordkeeping, and a state-certified mews and weathering house for the birds. The only bird species permitted for falcony in Connecticut are red-tailed hawks, merlins, prairie falcons, Harris's hawks, and infertile hybrid raptors. Evergreen Berry Farm is the only farm in Connecticut that employs falconry as a form of organic land control.

Zeke is the personal security guard for the thousands of berry bushes, and his domain is stunningly beautiful. On a gray March day more than thirty-two years ago, Bob Alex brought his fiancée to a dilapidated area of the Watertown countryside and asked, "Well, what do you think?" At first she thought she was going to pass out. He wasn't kidding! She married him anyway, and in 1979 Bob and Cathee Alex created Evergreen Berry Farm on the site of an abandoned corn field.

For more than a year they plowed, harrowed, removed more than 1,000 feet of rock walls, and conditioned the soil from the basic pH that corn requires to an acidic haven for blueberry bushes. Two weeks before their wedding, Bob and Cathee planted more than 7,000 two-year-old blueberry whips, and in 1984 Evergreen Berry Farm opened to the public for the first time for one day. Their inaugural berry crop fit onto a single, tiny scale.

Today the farm produces more than twenty-five tons of fruit and is open to the public every day throughout the summer with pick-your-own blueberry, raspberry, and blackberry orchards. More than 10,000 people visit Evergreen Berry Farm every year. "It's multigenerational," Cathee grins. "It's fun! Families have been coming for years. Grandparents bring their grandkids, and parents bring their kids for an inexpensive and enjoyable family outing."

Cathee, a soft-spoken audiology health practitioner, plays the roles of human resource manager, chemist, chief, cook, and bottle washer with Farmer Bob. Their three children haven't elected either to become or to raise future farmers. Their oldest is a second grade school teacher in New Jersey. In the middle is an auditory neuroscientist, and their youngest is working his way through medical school.

Although the Alexes' children don't work directly in the dirt every day, the reality is that farming and medicine are not unrelated. "I see a lot of parallels

1. In a mortar and pestle, mash the garlic, ginger, and sea salt to a paste. Set aside.

2. Puree blueberries in a blender. Add apple cider vinegar, ginger mash, and honey; puree until smooth.

3. Transfer the blueberry mixture to a heavy-bottomed 4-quart saucepan and bring to a gentle simmer. Continue to simmer, stirring often, for about 10 minutes, or until the liquid has reduced by half.

4. Add dark beer, stirring constantly until the sauce fizzes and bubbles and would overflow the saucepan if left unattended, about 5 minutes.

5. Remove from heat and allow mixture to cool to room temperature. Store in refrigerator in a tightly sealed container for up to 4 weeks. Can be frozen or canned in jars, adding more apple cider vinegar as necessary to adjust the acidity.

6. Use as a barbecue sauce on grilled food. Also makes a great dipping sauce for just about anything else you can think of!

with maintaining the health of the human body relative to maintaining the health of a field," Cathee points out. "Overall health and nutrition . . . it's all the same game."

Zeke's Blueberry BBQ Sauce

SERVES 4

2 teaspoons minced garlic
3 tablespoons minced fresh ginger
2 tablespoons sea salt
1 quart blueberries
¾ cup apple cider vinegar
¼ cup honey
½ cup dark beer

Evergreen Berry Farm
Bubbling Summer Casserole

SERVES 4

3 tablespoons butter, divided
1 large red onion, sliced thin
½ teaspoon sea salt
4 cups shredded fresh spinach
1 tablespoon fresh ginger, minced
1 cup raspberries
½ cup dry white wine
½ cup low-sodium chicken broth
3 teaspoons minced fresh dill
¼ cup fresh goat cheese
Sea salt and pepper to taste
1 pound yellow summer squash, sliced ¼ inch thick
1 pound zucchini, sliced ¼ inch thick

1. Heat oven to 400°F. Heat 2 tablespoons of the butter in a 12-inch skillet over medium heat. Sauté the onion and the ½ teaspoon sea salt until the onion is soft and browned around the edges. Add spinach, ginger, and raspberries, and continue to cook until the greens are wilted and the raspberries mash down into a paste. Spread mixture evenly over the bottom of a 9 x 13-inch baking dish. Set aside.

2. Melt the remaining tablespoon of butter in the skillet. Stir in the wine, broth, and dill, scraping the bottom of the pan to loosen browned bits. Whisk in the goat cheese. Season to taste with sea salt and pepper and set aside.

3. Shingle the slices of squash and zucchini in alternating rows over the onions. The slices will be nearly vertical. Sprinkle with black pepper. Pour the wine and goat cheese sauce evenly over the squash.

4. Bake until the squash has softened and the sauce is rich and bubbly, about 40 to 45 minutes. Serve hot.

FREUND'S FARM MARKET

324 Norfolk Rd., East Canaan, CT 06024 | (860) 824-0650 | www.freundsfarmmarket.com

Matthew Freund, the youngest of five siblings, operated his family's first farm stand from an old door set up on two hay bales under a maple tree. Upon returning to the farm after college, Matt was swept off his feet by a vigorous and stunningly beautiful Theresa, who has taken the farm market stand to a whole new level. Today Freund's Farm Market is a charming operation offering catering, locally produced food, award-winning take-out deli and bakery goods made with locally produced ingredients, 15,000 square feet of extensive greenhouses with setting plants and hydroponic tomatoes, and a garden for your local food pleasure.

Not only a smart capitalist, Theresa also shines through in her community-nominated position as the go-to gal for rescued animals, including chicks, lambs, and whatever else happens to be in need of a little extra TLC. While Matt tends to the 600 acres comprising Freund's Farm, most of which is preserved, the 250 cattle that are rotationally grazed, and his various inventions and projects, Theresa runs to the commercial

Matt and Theresa Freund

kitchen to start the day's baking and to throw open the doors of the store.

"We get up in the morning and I go out the front door," Matt says. "She goes out the back." This is a family agricultural operation in full swing.

Matt's grandfather, a Russian immigrant renamed Joe Brown at Ellis Island, first set foot in the northwest corner of Connecticut in the 1930s. The day Matt and Theresa got married, Matt walked into the house where he was born, took the bar out of the closet where his clothes hung, and walked down the road between the fields to his honeymoon house—which originally belonged to Grandpa Joe. Switching houses with his father again after his mother died, Matt has proceeded to raise his three daughters and one son in the same house he was born in.

Matt Freund always finds time for innovative inventions. Smart and ingenious, Matt's methane digester is a revolutionary poo-eating machine. The cow manure is heated to the temperature of the cow's stomach, and as it boils and bubbles away, methane gas is created. Gas is burned in a boiler, creating a scenario where poo from Matt's own cows heats the hot water tanks, the barns, the farm stand—even his house.

Matt is also the mastermind behind the biodegradable "CowPots," also made from the farm's recycled and treated cow manure. CowPots are seed-starter pots, an alternative to plastic and peat pots, and can be used as "pots you plant." With the methane burner and the CowPots, Matt has invented truly environment-saving ways to utilize products from the not very pleasant

backside of farming. I affectionately called him the king of . . . ahem . . . that stuff. And he is.

Matt and Theresa offer farm tours and hands-on activities for schoolchildren. Kids meet the newborn calves, milk the cows, and participate in a hands-on snack time where they pick popcorn kernels from dried ears of corn and make the tasty treat themselves. This direct engagement allows students to see first-hand how cows live, what they eat, how they're cared for, and how they produce milk. Matt and Theresa believe such encounters will pass along farming knowledge that's in danger of being lost to the youngest members of our society.

Matthew and Theresa Freund are agricultural entrepreneurs of the highest order. They absolutely love their land, and I am curious to see what will be in their next inventive bucket of surprises.

Freund's Farm Market Butter Roasted Asparagus

SERVES 4

    3 tablespoons unsalted butter
    2 pounds medium asparagus
    Sea salt and freshly ground pepper

Melt butter in a large 12- to 14-inch skillet. Add the asparagus, salt, and pepper. Roll the asparagus back and forth in the pan until browned on all sides. Serve warm.

Matt & Theresa's Carrot Bran Muffins

MAKES 12 MUFFINS

1¼ cups all-purpose flour
¼ cup whole wheat flour
1¼ teaspoons baking powder
½ teaspoon baking soda
¾ teaspoon sea salt
1¼ teaspoons ground cinnamon
¾ teaspoon ground allspice
½ teaspoon ground nutmeg
2 cups shredded carrots
1 cup plus 3 tablespoons buttermilk
3 tablespoons unsulphured molasses
2 teaspoons vanilla extract
¼ cup sour cream
7 tablespoons unsalted butter, softened
½ cup packed dark brown sugar
3 large eggs
1½ cups wheat bran
1 cup raisins

1. Preheat oven to 375°F.

2. In a medium bowl, combine flours, baking powder, baking soda, sea salt, and spices. In a separate bowl combine carrots, buttermilk, molasses, vanilla, and sour cream.

3. In the bowl of an electric mixer, beat butter until light and fluffy, about 1 to 2 minutes. Add brown sugar and increase speed to high. Beat mixture until combined and fluffy. Add the eggs, one at a time, beating thoroughly after each addition. Reduce the speed to low and slowly beat in the buttermilk-carrot mixture. Increase speed to medium low and add the flour mixture until incorporated and slightly curdled looking. Scrape down the sides of the bowl if necessary. Remove from the mixer, and add bran and raisins.

4. Spoon muffin mixture into a greased muffin tin or into cupcake papers, dividing evenly.

5. Bake until a toothpick inserted into the center of a muffin draws out only a few moist particles, about 25 minutes. Set on a wire rack to cool for 5 minutes before removing muffins from tin. Serve warm.

Note: This recipe is surprisingly agile. Feel free to use raw shredded zucchini, parsnips, or apples or cooked pureed pumpkin, squash, or other vegetables. If you'd like to add fresh fruit like blueberries, eliminate the raisins and add 1 to 2 cups fresh fruit. Surprisingly, parsnips and blackberries are perfect together in these muffins.

Laurel Ridge Grass Fed Beef

66 Wigwam Rd., Litchfield, CT 06759 | (860) 567-8122 | www.lrgfb.com

John Morosani welcomed his son Dan back to the states with a feast of slowly roasted beef shank raised directly on the soil surrounding their home. Capt. Dan Morosani served with a fifteen-man Marine unit in Diyala Province, north and east of Baghdad, as well as with Dani, a Shia Iraqi citizen. Dani is a remarkably peaceful person who tried to emigrate to the United States before the invasion. When that attempt failed, he served fifty-six months straight in his war-torn country as Captain Morosani's combat interpreter. Now performing more peaceful duties side by side with John at Laurel Ridge Farm, Dani has integrated perfectly into this American family that's still celebrating the safe return of their son.

John's father emigrated from Switzerland to teach skiing and settled instead into dairy farming. I didn't ask why. Nearly fifty years later, John enjoys bringing cows back onto his parent's property—the land upon which he was raised. An investment and financial guru, he stepped forth into agriculture by starting with a few milking cows, thinking that he'd restart his father's dairy operation. It didn't take John long to get inspired to raise grass-fed beef instead. Today Laurel Ridge Farm produces grass-fed beef and pastured pork and poultry.

John Morosani speaks so quietly and with a voice perfectly attuned to a lifetime career in radio, it is easy to wonder if perhaps you're accidentally making too much noise. This unpretentious whiz kid is deeply knowledgeable about Connecticut's agriculture, yet always struggling to find ethical and adequate animal processing operations.

Since most support services that sustain agricultural operations, such as an adequate supply of large animal veterinarians and slaughterhouses, have gone out of business, John hopes the creation of Laurel Ridge Farm and others like it will help spur growth in these service areas for the local food business.

"As more and more consumers want local food, there will be people out there increasing the size of their herds, like us." John says. "The more we can produce, the greater the demand for a processing facility within the state. That, in turn, benefits the consumer. The system will build on itself."

Unique to Laurel Ridge Farm are the 50,000-plus daffodils scattered about the rolling hillsides, drawing thousands to walk the property in wonder every spring. Envisioning the sea of daffodils in Wordsworth's poem, in 1941 John's mother negotiated a particularly rocky slope away from her husband's grazing lands and planted more than 10,000 daffodil bulbs. Every year until her death she split, halved, and replanted the bulbs, single-handedly creating her own luscious crowd of yellow-and-white flowers fluttering and dancing in the spring breeze.

The Morosani family feasts together very well. "It's really nice to be able to produce your own food," John says. "Now, if we could just get the vineyards going."

LAUREL RIDGE
GRASS FED BEEF
www.LRGFB.com
860-567-8122

John Morosani

Laurel Ridge Black Bean Soup

SERVES 8–10

> 1 pound dried black beans, picked over and rinsed
> 2 quarts water
> 6 cups chicken stock
> ¾ pound red potato, peeled and diced
> 2 ham hocks
> 2 cups chopped tomatoes
> 1 cup chopped onion
> ½ cup cilantro stems, bound with a rubber band
>   or string
> 1 teaspoon dried thyme
> 1 teaspoon sea salt
> ½ cup olive oil
> 3 garlic cloves, minced
> 3 tablespoons red wine vinegar
> Sea salt to taste
> Dash Tabasco

1. Put the beans in a large pot; cover with cold water and let stand for 1 hour. Drain the beans and rinse the pot.

2. Combine the beans, water, stock, potatoes, ham hocks, tomatoes, onion, cilantro stems, thyme, and sea salt in the rinsed pot and bring to a boil. Reduce the heat to low and cook, stirring occasionally, until the beans are tender and the soup has thickened, about 2½ hours. Remove the cilantro stems and discard.

3. Transfer 3 cups of the beans to a food processor, and puree until smooth. Stir the puree back into the soup. (If the soup is too thick, thin with a little water.) Stir in the olive oil, garlic, and vinegar; season with salt and Tabasco and bring to a gentle boil. Serve hot.

Captain Dan's Homecoming Beef Shanks

SERVES 4

1 teaspoon fennel seeds, toasted
1 teaspoon caraway seeds, toasted
2 cloves garlic
1 teaspoon sea salt
4 beef shanks, about 6 ounces each
2 teaspoons freshly ground pepper
1 cup flour
3 tablespoons oil or lard
2 cups medium-dice onions
1 cup medium-dice carrots
1 cup medium-dice turnips
1 cup red wine
2 quarts low-sodium chicken stock
3 bay leaves
2 tablespoons fresh thyme leaves
¼ cup chopped parsley

1. In a mortar and pestle, mash fennel and caraway seeds, garlic, and sea salt into a thick paste. Rub over beef shanks. Cover and marinate for at least 4 hours. Add pepper to the flour, and set aside.

2. In a 10-quart stockpot or braising pot, add the oil and heat over high heat. Dredge the beef shanks through the flour. Sear the shanks in the hot oil for 2 to 3 minutes on each side, or until very brown all the way around. Remove the shanks and set aside.

3. Add the onions, carrots, and turnips and sauté until browned. Deglaze the pan with red wine, scraping the bottom and sides to loosen the browned bits.

4. Add the stock and bring the liquid to a boil. Reducing to a simmer, add the shanks, bay leaves, and thyme. Continue to cook for about 2 hours over low to medium heat, basting the shanks often. Do not allow the liquid to boil. Cook until the sauce has a stewlike consistency and the meat starts to fall off the bone. Garnish with parsley and serve warm.

LOCAL FARM

22 Popple Swamp Rd., Cornwall Bridge, CT 06754 | (860) 672-0229 | http://rlocalfarm.com

Asking if it would be safe to walk out into the fields and closer to the dairy herd will yield as dumbfounded a look from Debra Tyler as if you'd just spoken to her in an obscure Yugoslavian dialect. It doesn't take long to realize that the fences at Local Farm serve to keep the cattle from wandering about on the road and function less as a mandated bovine-human species blockade. Plodding through the pasture grasses behind a barefoot Margaret and her mother, Debra, who is wearing a homemade dress and bonnet and swooping to pick Queen Anne's lace, one can see why these proprietors of raw milk would have reacted that way.

Among the bovines, oxen in training Jigger and Jolly are clearly happy to have the full, loving attention of these two selfless ladies. While the cows get milked, Jigger and Jolly will haul hay in the winter, till the garden in spring, and undertake other chores normally relegated to a gas-filled tractor.

Debra's mission is to work with what she's been given to unveil a heaven on Earth, and Local Farm clearly embodies her personal ideals. She finds great pleasure in doing something for herself rather than jumping from job to job to earn money for the sole purpose of buying things. She teaches Old World life skills workshops through the nonprofit Motherhouse, reminding attendees that they don't need to depend on retail stores for their survival and that food, clothing, and shelter can all be acquired from surrounding natural resources. She teaches canning, spinning, keeping cows or goats or chickens, bread making, and more—skills otherwise known as homesteading. Debra created the Motherhouse to celebrate mothers, cherish and support the feminine, and force us to slow down in this rat-race life.

Local Farm, set upon the stunning hills overlooking the Mohawk Valley in Cornwall Bridge, also sports a bovine boarding service that allows other farming families to take vacations. Only one other farm in Connecticut has been in the business of raw milk longer than Debra, and buying her raw milk requires that you call

Debra and Margaret Tyler

ahead to ensure that she has the necessary quantities. As for the controversy surrounding raw milk and the threat of potentially terminating legislation, Debra says, "Well, that's why I teach people how to produce milk themselves. There's only one milk better than what I can produce here, and that is milk from your own cow."

Guardian of the lost scrolls of homesteading, Debra reminds us of the magic of turning grass into energy, milk, or meat—an ability humans will never evolve to acquire. But cows can—slowly wrapping their

tongues around the grass, ripping it so that the roots aren't damaged.

The words "serenity" and "dairy farm" are seldom seen together in a sentence. Local Farm is an exception. At a time when industrial milking operations exterminate milking cows before they reach the age of four, Alisa, the first Jersey inhabitant of Local Farm, passed away just a few years ago at the ripe age of twenty-two. It's probably safe to say that she liked it here.

Local Farm Chilled Cucumber Soup

SERVES 4

> 6 cups peeled, seeded, and coarsely chopped cucumbers
> 2 yellow bell peppers, diced
> 1 clove garlic, sliced
> 1½ cups whole milk
> 1 cup whole-milk yogurt
> ½ cup sour cream
> ½ cup freshly squeezed grapefruit juice
> 1 tablespoon minced lemon zest
> 2 tablespoons minced fresh mint
> 1 tablespoon minced fresh dill
> 1 tablespoon minced fresh chives
> Sea salt and pepper

Combine all ingredients in bowl. Working in batches, puree the ingredients in a blender until very smooth. Transfer the soup to the refrigerator until well chilled and flavors have set, at least 2 hours. Season to taste with salt and pepper; serve cold.

Debra's Farmer Fortifying Cookies

SERVES 4

> 1½ cups old-fashioned peanut butter
> ½ cup butter
> 1½ cups packed brown sugar
> 3 eggs
> 1 teaspoon vanilla extract
> 4½ cups quick-cooking oats
> ½ cup ground flax seed meal
> 2 teaspoons baking soda
> 2 cups dried fruit and nuts, in any variety and
>   combination

1. Preheat oven to 350°F.

2. Using an electric mixer, cream together the peanut butter, butter, and brown sugar. Add eggs one at a time to the creamed mixture, beating after each addition. Beat in vanilla extract.

3. In a separate bowl, combine the oats, flax, and baking soda. Add to the creamed mixture.

4. Stir in dried fruit and nuts or just about anything you desire: shredded coconut, chocolate chips, etc.

5. Drop by the spoonful onto an ungreased cookie sheet and bake for 12 to 14 minutes. Cool on rack and serve with a frosty glass of fresh milk.

EALTHY · STAY HEALTHY

ALDINGFIELD FARM
24 East Street, Washington, CT

FRESH
VEGGIES

WALDINGFIELD FARM

24 East St., Washington, CT 06793 | (860) 868-7270 | www.waldingfieldfarm.com

Three brothers in their thirties are to blame for eighty-five varieties of 25,000 certified organic heirloom tomato plants nestled atop twenty acres of rolling hills in Washington, Connecticut. Fourteen years ago Dan Horan started Waldingfield Farm on his parents' estate, having never planted a seed in his life—a bold move for a recent college graduate who really just wanted to own his own business. Today Dan, Quincy, and Patrick Horan are entering their twentieth growing season at Waldingfield Farm.

You'll find screenplay writer Quincy and his twin brother, Patrick, at the helm of day-to-day farm operations—churning out more than one hundred varieties of vegetables, stocking the farm stand, packaging CSA shares, or delivering produce to markets or restaurants. With the advantage of family members as shareholders, these boys can draw on their expertise, advice, and support when they need it.

Quincy's knowledge of the land is unparalleled, while Patrick's focus is on marketing, sales, and operations. Dan's expertise as a food retail specialist completes the cross-spectrum team of brothers that stewards Waldingfield Farm today. In addition to its renowned status as an heirloom tomato producer, Waldingfield Farm is also famous for its organic greens and peas.

The job of agriculture must be profitable, and this small farm—like all others—occasionally strains the brothers' relationship as they struggle to keep Waldingfield Farm lucrative. Referring to the remarkably diverse personalities among them and the recent devastating tomato blight, Quincy admits, "We're a team. But sometimes, at the end of the day, it can get a little tight."

Purchased in 1917, the family estate was first farmed by the current owners when Dan put the first seedlings in the soil in 1990. Their agricultural production started with just one acre, and the brothers slowly began reclaiming the parcels of property leased to neighboring corn growers. Calling themselves "farmer pups," Patrick and Quincy are part of a burgeoning national young farmers' movement—pushing against the tide, since the current average age of a farmer in Connecticut is close to sixty-one.

Going against the tide of so many thirty-somethings leaving Connecticut, Patrick and Quincy would like to stick around and expand the farm, possibly to forty or fifty acres. They hope to become more at peace with the frantic risks the business of food production brings, becoming more efficient so that they can reach their goals. Quincy smiles a bit, adding that he wouldn't mind a girl and a house as well. Patrick was born first, by the way, making Quincy the baby of the family by four whole minutes. And, no, he didn't get extra cookies or special treatment as the youngest of siblings often do. "He got the brawn, I got the beauty," Patrick laughs. Quincy doesn't necessarily agree.

Chronically sleep deprived, these brothers always look forward to the monster Harvest Bash every fall, which celebrates the thousands of man-hours they've given to tuck yet one more year of farming under their belts. These young farmers are in it for the long haul, even though they still aren't particularly fond of hand-thinning and hand-weeding acres of beets. "Overall, it's a good life," Quincy says.

Farmer Quincy's Creamy Tomato Bisque

MAKES 3 QUARTS

2 tablespoons unsalted butter
1 medium onion, diced
3 cloves garlic, sliced
12 cups diced tomatoes
5 cups chicken stock
4 6-inch sprigs fresh oregano (plus more, minced, for garnish) bound by a rubber band or twine
½ cup whipping cream
Sea salt and fresh pepper to taste

1. Melt butter in a large soup kettle over medium-low heat. Add the onion and garlic; cook, stirring, until translucent, about 6 minutes.

2. Add the tomatoes, stock, and oregano sprigs. Bring to a boil and immediately reduce heat. Simmer gently until thickened, about 45 minutes. Remove oregano sprigs and discard.

3. Slowly add the whipping creams, stirring constantly. Season with salt and pepper to taste. Garnish with minced fresh oregano.

Patrick and Quincy Horan

Waldingfield's Cold Heirloom Soup

SERVES 4

> 16 ounces (2 cups) pureed heirloom tomatoes
> ½ ripe avocado
> Juice of one orange
> 1 tablespoon orange zest
> 2 teaspoons each sea salt and pepper
> ¼ teaspoon smoked paprika
> ½ cup freshly whipped cream, unsweetened

1. Cut heirloom tomatoes into chunks and, with their seeds and skins, puree them in a blender. Measure 16 ounces, or 2 cups.

2. Add avocado, orange juice, orange zest, sea salt, pepper, and paprika. Blend for about 2 minutes until well combined and the soup is frothy and creamy.

3. Place in the refrigerator for at least 1 hour to allow flavors to set.

4. Serve cold with a dollop of freshly whipped, unsweetened cream.

Chapter 4

MIDDLESEX COUNTY

DEERFIELD FARM

337 Parmelee Hill Rd., Durham, CT 06422 | (860) 301-7828 | www.deerfieldfarm.org

Melynda Naples is an inspiration. This twenty-something female farmer graduated from 4-H with an uphill battle on her hands: She wanted to be a farmer. At twenty-one, she didn't let her age or her gender get in the way of her dream.

Deerfield Farm, a small dairy farm, sells raw milk, yogurt, fresh cheeses, and succulent veal, all made by Melynda within five feet of the year-round, self-serve farm stand. The panoramic vista reveals her twenty cattle happily grazing down the slopes of rolling hillsides. The cows are outside most of the time on twenty acres of rotationally grazed pasture land surrounded by 200 acres of immaculate, undeveloped forest.

When this 260-acre leasable farm, one of the more scenic in all Connecticut, became available, Melynda fought for it. The start-up was exceedingly difficult, but after eight years in business, Melynda and her fiancé, Stu, have learned the ropes. Deerfield farm has settled into a more serene routine and pace. Soon Deerfield Farm will be expanding into mozzarella and ricotta, and they've started to make gelato on-site once again.

Melynda is a strong young woman who knows what she wants and isn't afraid of the hard work that it takes to succeed. Except for a brief interest in nutrition, she always wanted to be a farmer. She hated being inside and would rather have her hands on something more than a calorie-crunching calculator. "I realized that I'm more on the natural side of things," she says smiling sheepishly.

Melynda wants young people to know that farming is a viable career. She chafes at the advice given to the next generation that they need a "real job" and can only farm "on the side." She finds it beyond irritating that, in her experience, young people in 4-H are not encouraged to consider food production as a legitimate vocation.

As a woman, Melynda has found it difficult at times to go into a feed store and not have the older generation of agricultural pioneers dismiss her as not a "real farmer." Quick to laugh at the biases of the Old Guard and ripe with all the possibilities of youth, Melynda continues to host 4-H Clubs at Deerfield Farm. She shows members the wondrous agricultural possibilities in her own life, encouraging them to believe that accomplishing such dreams are possible. Almost single-handedly, Melynda is paving the way for the next generation of Connecticut farmers.

Melynda never gets up in the morning, dreading to go to work or to milk her cows. Her next dream? Hiring a farmhand, perhaps. "I wouldn't mind sleeping in from time to time—well, maybe just once."

What a pleasure to watch her enjoying the fruits of her labor! It is gratifying to know that four-year-old Reba and two-year-old Gabrielle have such a renegade mom. I hope they've inherited her unsinkable spirit.

Deerfield Farm Macaroni & Cheese

SERVES 4

2 cups whole milk, plus more as needed to thin sauce
4 tablespoons melted butter
2 cups diced yellow summer squash
3½ tablespoons all-purpose flour
¼ teaspoon sea salt
Pepper to taste
½ cup shredded cheese
4 cups shredded fresh spinach
6 cups cooked pasta
Sea salt and pepper to taste

1. Warm milk in a small saucepan over low heat until hot but not boiling.

2. In a separate heavy-bottomed saucepan over medium heat, melt butter and sauté the summer squash until tender, about 2 minutes. Remove from heat and whisk in flour, stirring constantly for about 2 minutes. Do not let the flour brown.

3. Add ¼ cup of the hot milk and whisk vigorously with a wooden spoon. Repeat, adding more milk and scraping the roux from the sides of the pan. Return the pan to a very low heat, and slowly stir in the remaining milk.

4. Raise the heat to medium-low. Add the sea salt and cook, stirring constantly, until the sauce thickens to a consistency of thick heavy cream, about another 8 to 10 minutes. Remove pan from heat, and whisk in pepper and cheese. If necessary, thin the sauce with more milk.

5. Add fresh spinach to a colander. Drain freshly cooked pasta into that colander over the fresh spinach. Combine spinach and pasta and the cheese sauce in a serving bowl. Stir to combine and season with sea salt and pepper. Serve warm.

Farmer Melynda's Gingered Twice-Baked Potatoes

SERVES 4

> 4 russet potatoes (8 ounces each), scrubbed, dried, and
>   rubbed lightly with olive oil
> 2 tablespoons butter
> 2 teaspoons lemon zest
> 2 tablespoons finely grated fresh ginger
> ¼ teaspoon ground cinnamon
> 1 cup whole-milk yogurt
> 3 tablespoons fresh lemon juice

1. Preheat the oven to 400°F and bake potatoes on a foil-lined baking sheet until skin is crisp and pierces easily with a fork, about 1 hour. Transfer potatoes to a wire rack until cool enough to handle.

2. Cut each potato in half lengthwise. Use a small spoon to scoop out the cooked flesh into a medium bowl, leaving a ⅛-inch thickness of flesh in the shells. Return the shells to the oven on the baking sheet and allow to cook and crisp, about 10 minutes.

3. Heat the butter in a medium skillet over medium heat. Quickly sauté the lemon zest, ginger, and cinnamon for about 15 seconds, stirring continuously. Mix the cooked spices with the yogurt and lemon juice.

4. Mash the cooked potato flesh with a fork until smooth. Add ¼ cup of the yogurt mixture at a time, continuously mashing to yield a creamy texture.

5. Remove the potato shells from the oven and increase the oven setting to broil. Spoon ¼ of the yogurt and potato mixture into each shell, mounding slightly at the center. Return to oven and broil until brown and crisp on the top, about 10 minutes. Allow to cool for 10 minutes before serving.

Melynda Naples

Lyman Orchards

7 Lyman Rd., Middlefield, CT 06455 | (860) 349-1793 | www.lymanorchards.com

Lyman Orchards is known as one of the greatest agri-tourism meccas in all of Connecticut. It sports two championship eighteen-hole golf courses, corn and sunflower mazes, pick-your-own everything on tree or vine, an apple hunt, and a farm store that serves an outdoor breakfast just about every day. From strawberries in June to pumpkins in October, John Lyman's orchards provide a seasonal backdrop for myriad out-of-the-box activities. The year-round Apple Barrel Market showcases Lyman's signature products—including their award-wining Hi-Top Apple Pie—as well as Connecticut-grown fruits, vegetables, specialty products, cheeses, a full-service bakery and deli, and everything else one could possibly imagine. At their peak, Lyman Orchards provides more than 250 jobs. This is a farm stand on steroids.

Yet for all the hype and hoopla, John Lyman is a placid businessman—albeit an agribusinessman of ambitious grandeur. He is an eighth-generation farmer with the official title of executive vice president, yet despite that official and intimidating salutation, you can't help but like him. John has a deep commitment to the preservation of farmlands and open space—which, luckily for the town of Middlefield, under John's land stewardship won't be so quickly devoured by strip malls and asphalt.

After the Civil War, Lyman lands, property originally used for subsistence farming, became a commercial orchard. With 1,100 contiguous acres, the Lymans needed to diversify their business operation to remain profitable, and today they cultivate only 200 acres of pure, food-growing dirt. This agritourism diversification has allowed the family to preserve the rest of the land, keeping it as open, undeveloped space.

The Lyman's commercial pie business, with accounts in more than seven states, is a pioneer among Connecticut farms, generating income during the seven non-

John Lyman

growing months of the year and mitigating the risk of weather extremes that affect the farming industry as a whole. For all farmers in Connecticut, finding commercial production space continues to be a factor in the limited growth of prepared-food operations statewide.

With its four business divisions—orchards, golf courses, Apple Barrel Market, and commercial pies—Lyman Orchards is forging new ground in Connecticut agriculture. Family fun, great food, championship golf—this is one place an entire family could come and get lost for an entire day in myriad different adventures and activities. Whatever you choose to do, John will be there, smiling.

Lyman Orchard Veal Cutlets with Apple Cider Sauce

SERVES 4

4 thinly sliced veal cutlets, 3–4 ounces each

3 tablespoons extra virgin olive oil, divided

2 medium shallots, minced

1¼ cups apple cider

2 tablespoons apple cider vinegar

2 tablespoons Lyman's Jostaberry Preserves or red currant jelly

2 teaspoons minced parsley

2 tablespoons unsalted butter

Sea salt and pepper to taste

1. Preheat oven to 200°F. Season both sides of the veal cutlets with a tiny bit of sea salt and pepper. Heat 2 tablespoons of the olive oil in a 12-inch skillet over medium heat. Sauté the cutlets and cook, without moving them, until browned on the bottom, about 2 minutes. Flip cutlets and continue to cook until the second side is opaque, about 30 seconds. Transfer to a heatproof plate, cover loosely with foil, and transfer to the oven to keep warm.

2. To the hot skillet, add remaining tablespoon of olive oil and the shallots, cooking over medium heat until softened. Add cider and vinegar; bring to a simmer, scraping the bottom of the pan to loosen the browned bits. Simmer until reduced to ½ cup. Remove from heat; stir in preserves and parsley. Whisk in cold butter 1 tablespoon at a time. Adjust seasonings with sea salt and pepper, spoon over the cutlets, and serve immediately.

John Lyman's Peachy Bean Salad

SERVES 4

1½ pounds fresh cranberry or lima beans in their pods
2 tablespoons sea salt
2 cups peeled and diced fresh peaches
¼ cup extra virgin olive oil
1 tablespoon apple cider
2 tablespoons finely chopped basil
Sea salt and pepper to taste

1. Shell the beans and reserve. Bring 2 quarts of water to a rapid boil in a large pot. Add sea salt and beans and boil for 10 to 20 minutes, until the beans are no longer mealy when tasted.

2. Drain the beans in a colander and immediately toss in a bowl with the peaches, olive oil, apple cider, and basil. Cover tightly with plastic wrap to sweat the peaches and let cool to room temperature.

3. Season to taste with sea salt and pepper. Serve cold or at room temperature.

Staehly Farms

278 Town St., East Haddam, CT 06423 | (860) 873-9774 | www.staehlys.com

Kevin is pretty cute, his face still carrying the rounded vestiges of adolescence. Eager and bright, this baby-faced young man is a great spokesman for Staehly Farms.

His father, Chris Staehly, an aerospace engineer, decided to plant Christmas trees on their property, with the ulterior motive that he wouldn't need to spend so much time mowing the lawn. In 1985, their first year of operation, they sold just six trees. In frustration, Chris was ready to rip out the rest of the trees and go back to the humdrum chore of just cutting the grass. Well, he didn't, and the Staehly Farm operation continued to grow year after year—diversifying and expanding to the present.

Staehly Farm became a full-time operation when Chris's company sold its Connecticut aerospace division. Refusing to move to California, in 2002 Chris tapped the then fourth grader Kevin on the head and announced, "This family is going to become full-time farmers." Today this robust farm is managed by Chris, an aerospace engineer; Kevin, currently studying marine biology in Tacoma, Washington; and the lovely little Gail—mother, wife, and farm store manager.

Finding the small Staehly Farms stand means driving under the speed limit on busy Route 82, to the great dismay of impatient Connecticut drivers. This is one farm that ought not to be judged by its cover. Deceptively unassuming at first-glance, the Staehly property offers a sixty-six-acre orchard with apples and raspberries and seventy acres of Christmas trees—including their award-winning white pine—hidden behind a farm stand with its simple sign offering firewood for sale. Extensive greenhouses produce vegetables, plants, seedlings, and flowers. Their sawmill produces rough-cut wood products, landscape beams, and bean poles. Gail will greet you at the farm stand and offer you the best of locally produced foods from around the region.

Between deer, flooding, and droughts, the family has on multiple occasions lost entire acres of trees, enough to give any new farmer pause about continuing such one-sided, often-devastating, negotiations with Mother Nature. Instead, the Staehly family has grown closer, stronger, more determined, and more interdependent. With Chris and Gail's only child fledging off to college nearly 3,000 miles away, there is an air of both great sadness and sheer excitement. The secure fabric of this family unit—the farm tying each of them together with a glue nearly as strong as their shared biology—will be devoid of one of its members, and Staehly Farms will dearly miss Kevin. With a sidelong look at his silent father, Kevin says, "It'll be a long four years."

Chris, Kevin, and Gail Staehly

Kevin's Scallop Seviche

SERVES 4

1 pound bay scallops, sliced into ¼-inch disks
Juice of 3 limes
3 tablespoons minced cilantro
1 jalapeño pepper, seeded and minced (optional)
2 tablespoons honey
Juice of 2 lemons
1 cup fresh peas, shelled
1 apple, peeled and diced small
Sea salt and pepper to taste

1. Combine scallops, lime juice, cilantro, and jalapeño in a large bowl. Cover and refrigerate for at least 30 minutes, until the scallops turn opaque and are cooked through by the acid from the lime juice.

2. In a second bowl mix the honey and lemon juice. Pour over peas and apple and toss to combine. Refrigerate until needed.

3. To serve, mix pea and scallop mixtures. Season to taste with sea salt and pepper. Serve very cold.

Staehly Farms Pear Chestnut Puree

SERVES 6

40 fresh chestnuts, shelled and peeled
2 cups low-sodium chicken stock
2 teaspoons maple syrup
1 cinnamon stick
6 pears, cored and diced
2 tablespoons apple cider vinegar
½ cup butter
Sea salt and pepper to taste

1. Combine chestnuts, chicken stock, maple syrup, and cinnamon stick in a medium stockpot. Simmer over medium-low heat, covered, for about 45 minutes. Drain the chestnuts in a colander, reserving the liquid. Set chestnuts aside, discarding the cinnamon stick.

2. Dice the pears and immediately toss in the apple cider vinegar to prevent discoloration.

3. Melt the butter in the hot stockpot, and add the pears. Sauté until browned.

4. Puree the chestnuts and buttered pears in a food processor, adding just enough reserved cooking liquid to enable the blades to turn. Work the puree through a wide-mesh strainer with a wooden spoon into a serving dish. Season to taste with salt and pepper. Serve warm.

STARLIGHT GARDENS

54 Fowler Ave., Durham, CT 06422 | (860) 463-0166 | www.starlightgardensct.com

David and Ty Zemelsky, co-owners of Starlight Gardens, jumped off the proverbial agricultural cliff. They built four greenhouses almost overnight, yet both kept their other jobs for six months before David retired and began farming full-time. Little by little, they've continued to expand from growing only lettuce to raising arugula, spinach, red Russian kale, miner's lettuce, and now heirloom tomatoes—selling only to restaurants, ones they could not afford to frequent. Greens branched out into pea tendrils, and they are quickly approaching their twelfth year of farming. In their fifth year of operation, they began participating in farmers' markets, which now contribute to half their business.

An all-season farm, Starlight Gardens grows year-round throughout their extensive high-tunnel growing system. They believe in sustainably grown food without

supplemental heat, a practice that not only creates a zero carbon footprint but also improves the quality of the greens, which thrive and become sweeter in colder temperatures.

An ardent artist, Ty continues to paint, and it is her passion that affects all aspects of Starlight Gardens— an underlying driving force that informs the farm and their personal lives. The farm provides Ty with the opportunity to have other bodies around her on the property, easing the isolative nature of her work with paints and brushes.

David has reinvented himself many times. He has been the manager of his family's business, the Powder Ridge Ski Area; an eighth grade school teacher; and a licensed family therapist. He claims that farming has nothing to do with his other three lives, but it does. Working the soil and playing in the dirt is good therapy, indeed. Healthy food keeps kids strong and enables them to develop emotionally, and the list goes on. Purchasing food from Starlight Gardens provides not only a nutritional powerhouse but a set of well-seasoned listening ears as well.

Personally, both David and Ty are as continuously evolving as each season of plant rotations on their farm. As David notes, "At this point, we're pretty much at the top of our game. Don't get me wrong, there is so much more we can learn, but we've been able to establish ourselves as the go-to grower for heirloom tomatoes."

Why farming? It has gotten into their blood. Farming originally seemed, on paper at least, a bit of a good

David and Ty Zemelsky

idea—and perhaps a bit of a silly idea, Ty acknowledges. With no formal agricultural training, and with the purchase of their land first and creation of the farm on a whim, farming to the Zemelskys has become a science, an art, a political statement, and a social endeavor. They jumped in feet first, learned to swim, and became

one of the most recognizable and notable growers in Connecticut.

They profess that there is much more that they'd like to learn, more art they'd like to create, more hands they'd like to shake, more food they'd like to grow. No doubt there will be many more years of interactive dirt therapy to come.

Starlight Gardens Herb and Spice Salad

SERVES 4

> ½ teaspoon crushed fennel seeds
> ½ teaspoon crushed cumin seeds
> 1 small clove garlic
> ½ teaspoon sea salt
> 1 teaspoon coarsely chopped fresh thyme
> ¼ cup olive oil
> 3 tablespoons balsamic vinegar
> 2 large shallots, minced
> Pepper to taste
> 4 gigantic handfuls mixed salad greens: arugula, spinach, frisée, romaine, etc.

1. To make vinaigrette: Crush fennel and cumin seeds using a mortar and pestle. Add garlic, sea salt, and thyme, and continue to pound into a paste.

2. In small bowl whisk together olive oil and vinegar. Add shallots, pepper, and spice paste.

3. Toss with washed and dried salad greens and serve!

Farmer David's Hearty Beef Chili

SERVES 8

2 tablespoons extra virgin olive oil

2 onions, diced

2 red bell peppers, stemmed, seeded, and diced fine

4 tablespoons chili powder

1 tablespoon ground cumin

2 teaspoons ground coriander

½ teaspoon cayenne pepper

2 pounds ground beef

3 tablespoons flour

¼ cup low-sodium chicken broth

2 (15.5-ounce) cans dark red kidney beans, drained and rinsed

6 cups diced fresh tomatoes

¼ cup minced oregano

Sea salt and pepper to taste

1. Heat the oven to 300°F. Heat the oil in a large ovenproof Dutch oven over medium heat. Add the onions, peppers, chili powder, cumin, coriander, and cayenne pepper. Cook, stirring occasionally until the vegetables are soft and beginning to brown, about 10 minutes. Increase the heat to medium high and add half the meat. Cook until meat is no longer pink and just beginning to brown. Add the remaining ground beef and repeat.

2. Add the flour and stir, cooking until everything is evenly coated, about 2 minutes. Add the chicken broth and continue cooking until a sauce starts to form.

3. Add the beans, tomatoes, and oregano; bring to a boil.

4. Cover the pot and transfer to the oven. Cook for 1 hour. Remove the lid, and stir to redistribute the meat and beans. Cook uncovered until the beef is tender and the chili is dark, rich, and thickened, about 40 minutes. Season to taste with sea salt and pepper before serving.

Chapter 5
NEW HAVEN COUNTY

CECARELLI FARM

173 Old Post Rd., Northford, CT 06472 | (203) 484-0101

With 133 acres of preserved land in full production, Cecarelli Farm is one of the largest farms covered in this book. Such a large area of preserved farmland is exceedingly rare in New Haven County. Despite preserving 1,370 acres of farmland in 2009—a 100 percent increase over the previous year—the state of Connecticut is at only 30 percent of the goal it set in 1980 to preserve more than 130,000 acres statewide. At the current pace of preservation, and the rate at which farmland is being converted to nonfarm uses, it is becoming increasingly apparent that we may not reach our intended target.

Nelson Cecarelli and farm manager William

Preserving farmland is more than just purchasing development rights. Preservation advocates now play a role in helping make farming operations profitable. Protecting farmland also helps keep land affordable for future farmers and curbs the rising costs of farmland that, at its current escalation, will eventually push existing farmers out of their fields.

Before attending college, William, the farm manager, worked for Nelson Cecarelli, the third generation of his family to farm this land. After working indoors at a John Deere dealership, he realized that he'd much rather be farming—and back to the Cecarelli Farm he went. Now he doesn't dream of doing anything else.

Cecarelli Farm produces corn, peppers, eggplant, tomatoes, squash, lettuce, cabbage, peas, shell beans, and just about anything else an industrial farm would grow. With a packinghouse on site, they grow, pack, and then ship with refrigerated delivery trucks to farm stands, stores, and two distributers. They also have their own farm stand and sell their products to retail consumers through farmers' markets.

An Italian immigrant, Nelson Cecarelli's grandfather purchased a sequence of smaller farms in 1912 and slowly began combining them to create the large, three-section farm that we see today. With 200 to 400 tons of food produced per acre, Cecarelli Farm is a colossal

tycoon in local food production. But although the farm is industrial in size, every plant on all 133 acres is handpicked.

Nelson Cecarelli is a witty fellow, easing back in his chair to debate the politics of the way things are and the way things ought to be. He has a wicked grin— a bit mischievous—making one think that this once-youthful, perhaps James-Dean-wannabe bad boy is not totally grown up yet. Charming.

Cecarelli Farm Baked Corn Pudding

SERVES 8

2 tablespoons butter, melted
½ cup fresh bread crumbs
10–12 ears corn, husks and silk removed
¼ cup freshly squeezed orange juice
½ teaspoon sea salt
2 eggs, beaten
3 tablespoons minced chives
2 teaspoons minced orange zest
¾ cup heavy cream

1. Heat oven to 350°F. Grease a 2-quart casserole dish with the melted butter. Add bread crumbs, and roll them around in the dish to evenly coat the bottom and sides.

2. Grate each ear of corn on a coarse box grater to extract 3 cups of corn pulp. Thoroughly mix corn pulp with orange juice, sea salt, eggs, chives, and orange zest. Add heavy cream, and toss gently to combine.

3. Immediately pour corn mixture into prepared dish and bake until the center is barely set, 45 to 50 minutes. Serve hot or warm.

Nelson's Arugula Radish Salad

SERVES 4

5 teaspoons freshly squeezed lime juice
¼ tablespoon Dijon mustard
½ teaspoon ground coriander, toasted in a dry skillet for 30 seconds
3 tablespoons fresh thyme
¼ teaspoon sea salt
¼ teaspoon ground black pepper
3 tablespoons olive oil
1½ cups diced oranges
5 radishes, quartered and sliced thin
4 cups baby arugula

1. In a small bowl, whisk lime juice, mustard, coriander, thyme, sea salt, and pepper until combined. Whisking constantly, gradually add the oil to form a vinaigrette.

2. Combine oranges, radishes, and arugula; toss gently to combine. Add vinaigrette and toss to combine again. Serve immediately.

GAZY BROTHERS FARM

391 Chestnut Tree Hill Rd., Oxford, CT 06478 | (203) 723-8885 | www.gazybrothersfarm.net

Ed and Lexi Gazy are, how shall I put it, too cute for words—a description that is too sugary for a greeting card, let alone this type of book. Well, there you are. I've said it. These proprietors of the eighty-acre Gazy Brothers Farm, established in 1910 by Grandma and Grandpa Gazsi, are among the hardest working, most respected, and singularly devoted land stewards in Connecticut. Theirs is a century farm, soon to celebrate its one-hundredth year in farm production.

Every day there are three generations toiling on the Gazy Brothers' land. If any of the four Gazy children decide to take over the farm, they'll be the fourth generation of this family to grow our local food. "They have to have their heart in farming, you know," Ed says. "They'll do what feels right to them." Time will tell.

Ed's ninety-year-old father, Joseph Gazy, sits quietly outside against the barn in his flannel jacket and hat, resting with nothing in particular to say, a few empty beer cans at his feet. He deserves to rest! This elder of the Gazy tribe created the Gazy Brothers Farm—providing a livelihood and years of hands-on training to Ed and Lexi—and has been a beacon of leadership for his children's children. (At the writing of this book, a frantic and unusually downbeat phone call from Lexi brought forth the realization that perhaps as early as the first snows of winter, it will be only Ed, Lexi, and their children who remain.)

Gazy Brothers Farm is successful at what it does: running a thriving CSA program with more than 250 customers and growing and participating in more than thirteen farmers' markets. They have a small but vibrant stand at the farm, and you can often catch Lexi zipping around the state delivering produce. All in the wild throes of teenager-dom, Dominic, Rose, Nicholas, and Albert roll up their sleeves and help out, making this farm intrinsic to the fiber of their family unit.

To feed people is their passion. The Gazys love watching the transformation of seed to stem to leaf to

Lexi, Joseph, and Ed Gazy

bulb to casserole, and they enjoy the little things like driving around in the brand-new tractor—a tribute to their frugal habits and long-term business strategy. Dreaming of grandkids crawling about on the farm some day, a long-term vision, and clearing the land for an orchard, a short-term vision, Ed and Lexi are undemanding, straightforward, and gently honest.

"If you keep eating, we'll keep growing!" Lexi says.

Gazy Brothers Farm Shaved Parsnip Salad

SERVES 4

> 4 large carrots, peeled
> 1½ tablespoons lemon juice
> 4 large parsnips, peeled
> 3 tablespoons olive oil
> 2 teaspoons roasted garlic
> 3 tablespoons fresh thyme leaves
> Sea salt and pepper to taste

1. With a vegetable peeler, peel carrots into shavings. Toss carrots in lemon juice and pepper to taste. Set aside at room temperature for 1 hour.

2. With a vegetable peeler, peel parsnips into shavings. Toss parsnips with olive oil, roasted garlic, and thyme. Set aside at room temperature for 1 hour.

3. Just prior to serving, combine the carrots and parsnips. Season with sea salt to taste and serve.

Joe Gazy's Rosemary Turnip Ratatouille

SERVES 6–8

Marinade

⅓ cup minced rosemary leaves

¾ teaspoon dried lavender (optional)

3 cloves garlic, sliced

2 teaspoons orange zest

2 teaspoons sea salt

⅓ cup extra virgin olive oil

3 tablespoons fresh lemon juice

3 tablespoons fresh orange juice

Vegetables

3 pounds carrots, halved and sliced

3 pounds turnips, diced to the same size as the carrots

1. Preheat oven to 350°F. With a mortar and pestle or in a blender, blend the rosemary, lavender, garlic, orange zest, and sea salt to a course paste. Transfer to a small bowl and blend in the olive oil, lemon juice, and orange juice.

2. Pour the mixture over carrots and turnips that have been placed in large (16 x 9 inches) roasting or casserole dish. Toss to combine. (*Note:* Lots of air space is necessary for browning, so if the vegetables are piled too high and too deep, use two roasting or casserole dishes as needed, baking them together. Use sheet trays if desired.)

3. Bake for at least 2 hours, stirring occasionally to rotate the turnips and to ensure browning on all sides. Roast until carrots and turnips have released their juices and are brown and starting to crisp. Serve warm

Note: This marinade is brilliant with lamb, duck, pork, quail, chicken, turkey, or beef. Will marinate up to 3 pounds of food. Marinate meat for at least 12 hours and up to 3 days.

MID-SOUND FISHERIES

50 Maple St., Branford, CT 06405 | (203) 627-5173

Rumor has it that Arlene's Lobster Shack in Branford is an award-winning food truck with brown-butter lobster rolls that draws travelers from nearly all fifty states—so good that you'll drive out of your way for another one. A few napkins later, well, maybe more than a few, I am pleased to announce that this story is completely factual.

A bit understated next to the vivacious and perfectly coifed Arlene is a wizened gentleman resting comfortably under a shade umbrella. Meet Arlene's husband, Nick Crismale, of Mid-Sound Fisheries.

Nick has provided us with fresh seafood for more than thirty-eight years, formerly as a lobster fisherman before the West Nile virus pesticide sprayed in New York in September 1999 leached into Long Island Sound, compliments of Hurricane Floyd, and ravaged the lobster population. "Lobsters are basically bugs. Pesticides are indiscriminate," Nick says. "They're basically just like mosquitoes. They are from the same phylum: arthropods."

When the pesticides decimated the lobsters, Nick turned to clams and oysters to supplement the family's income and keep them viable on the water. He's optimistic, though. He believes that the bugs we love to eat so much are coming back. It will just take time.

With three clam boats parked at the end of the Branford River as it flows out to sea, Mid-Sound Fisheries uses new technology designed by Nick to process both clams and oysters directly out on the water. The *Mighty Maxx* looks less like a typical boat and more like a two-pronged fork with a gaping hole right down the center over which to sort, count, and bag our favorite seafood.

A trained law enforcement officer with eight years on the police force, Nick believes that the only regrets that we have in life are the chances we didn't take or the dreams we didn't follow. He always wanted to spend his days out on the sea, and he thanks Arlene for having

the patience to allow him to try out fishing as a full-time profession. Cold turkey, throwing his hat into the wind, Nick left the force saying, "What the hell! We're going a lobsterin' today." People in the know say that once the water has bitten you, you can't wait to get back off the land.

Now that Arlene is retired and their two daughters have fledged, she spends her days down on the docks with Nick in the family business of foraging for seafood and then cooking it up for our dining pleasure. The clams, oysters, and lobster that Nick finds go directly to Arlene's prep tables. In addition to lobster rolls and steamed littlenecks, Nick, who professes not to know how to cook, makes a faultless broth-based clam chowder that rivals the best of any chef.

Load up on fresh seafood from Long Island Sound. Stay for lunch. This pristine food-lover's paradise tucked between a train station and the abandoned warehouse buildings of the old iron foundry is a kind-hearted haven of which legends are made.

Nick and Arlene Crismale

Fisherman Nick's Stovetop Clambake

SERVES 4

> 4 pounds littleneck or cherrystone clams, washed and
>   scrubbed
> 1 pound kielbasa, sliced into ⅓-inch-thick rounds
> 1 pound new or red potatoes, scrubbed and cut into
>   1-inch pieces
> 4 medium ears corn, with silk and all but the last
>   layer of husk removed
> 4 live lobsters, about 1 pound each
> 1 raw egg, washed
> 8 tablespoons salted butter, melted
> 1 lemon, wedged

1. Place clams in a large piece of cheesecloth and tie the ends together. Set aside.

2. In a tall and narrow 8-quart stockpot, layer the sliced kielbasa on the bottom. Layer the sack of clams, the potatoes, the corn, and the lobsters on top in that order, from bottom to top. Top with a raw egg in its shell.

3. Cover stockpot and place over high heat. Cook until the potatoes are tender, the lobsters are red, and the egg has cooked through. Break open the egg at about 18 minutes to check for doneness. When the egg has cooked, so has the lobster.

4. Remove the pot from heat. Remove all the ingredients and arrange on a large platter; pour the cooking liquid from the pot on top. Remove the last layer of cornhusk and the clams from the cheesecloth.

5. Serve with melted butter and lemon wedges.

Arlene's Nontraditional New England Clam Chowder

SERVES 4

> 7 pounds chowder clams, washed and scrubbed
> 4 slices thick-cut bacon, cut into ¼-inch pieces
> 1 large sweet onion, chopped medium
> 2 tablespoons flour
> 1½ pounds red potatoes, scrubbed and cut into
>   ½-inch dice
> 1 cup raw corn kernels, cut from the cob
> 1 large bay leaf
> 1 teaspoon fresh thyme leaves
> 1 cup heavy cream
> 2 tablespoons minced parsley
> Sea salt and pepper to taste

1. Bring 3 cups water to a boil in a large stockpot. Add clams and cover with a tight-fitting lid. Stirring once, steam the clams until they open, about 5 minutes.

2. Transfer the clams to a large bowl. Reserve all but 1 tablespoon of the steaming broth to a bowl. Holding the clams over the broth, cut them from the shell and transfer the meat to a cutting board. Mince the clams and set aside.

3. Fry the bacon in a medium stockpot over medium heat until crispy. Add the onion and cook until softened. Add the flour and stir until lightly colored, about 1 minute. Gradually whisk in the reserved clam-steaming broth, stirring continuously. Add the potatoes, corn, bay leaf, and thyme; simmer until potatoes are tender, 10 to 15 minutes.

4. Remove half the soup to a blender and puree. Pour the puree back into the pot with the nonpureed soup; add the clams, cream, parsley, and sea salt and pepper to taste. Bring to a simmer and serve immediately.

Mountaintop Mushroom

300 Chase River Rd., Waterbury, CT 06722 | (860) 919-5264

You might get lost coming to Mountaintop Mushroom. First you must snake your way through a maze of abandoned commercial buildings on the back side of Waterbury until you find a weedy parking lot at the base of an old textile mill. There you'll find Gregg Wershoven and Josh and Joe, his right- and left-hand partners in this fungal empire.

This is not a typical farm. Gregg is brilliantly reusing old, abandoned warehouse space to produce food. Mushrooms grow in low light and humidity, and Gregg grows without commercial temperature-humidity-controlled equipment in a foreclosed building of which Gregg was asked to be property manager. One night he was sitting in the basement overseeing the repair of the fire sprinklers. At 3:00 a.m. an idea struck this independent contractor with aching knees. He told himself, *I have to find something else in life. I'm going to be fifty years old. I can't keep crawling around on the floor laying tile.*

He jokes a bit about the other ideas that crossed his mind—such as the illegal crops that could be grown in an unattended warehouse basement. With orange jumpsuits not being the right color for his complexion, and not liking the idea of waving to his three daughters from the front page of *Arrested News,* he happily settled on cultivating mushrooms.

Books, libraries, and the World Wide Web helped this nouveau farmer transition an idea and a dusty basement into a commodity fought over by chefs across Connecticut. Chef Scott Miller from Max's Oyster Bar and Chef Nick Mancini from La Tavola kept Gregg encouraged as he dealt with the learning curve of sporadic production.

Demand for locally grown mushrooms far exceeds supply, and Gregg is struggling to expand his operations to become one of the premium growers in Connecticut and Massachusetts. "We're still rudimentary." Gregg says. "I'm spending a great deal of time marinating over the next level of commercial operations."

Josh and Joe still pasteurize straw for the mushroom-growing medium the old-fashioned way—by boiling it in two fifty-five-gallon drums. Commercial operations have forty-bale steam rooms, allowing them to pasteurize 90 percent more straw for the same investment, and thus grow more mushrooms faster. Boilers, steamers, and moving floors are the types of capital equipment needed to bring Mountaintop Mushroom to the next level of quantity production—highlighting the need to continuously infuse capital into the burgeoning local food movement.

Mushrooms are a bit funky anyway. They're not particularly lovely to look at, and they seem to pop up where we would really rather they didn't grow. Yet cultivating mushrooms for harvest is a highly tuned skill.

Gregg's getting there. His eyes glowed in his tired face as we spent some time dreaming of the massive scale of food production, mushrooms and otherwise, that could be generated from this abandoned commercial property. He is a pioneer in regenerative farming—utilizing old, unused spaces for new-scale food production. His mental wheels spin with excitement.

Gregg's Mushroom & Duck Confit Salad

SERVES 4

4 gigantic handfuls of mixed salad greens: arugula, frisée, romaine, etc.

2 confit duck legs (See Soeltl Farm's Donna's Duck Confit on page 155.)

1 pound fresh mushrooms, cut into bite size pieces
3 tablespoons duck fat from the confit
3 tablespoons olive oil
1 tablespoon freshly squeezed lemon juice
Sea salt and pepper to taste

1. Wash and dry the salad greens.

2. Pull the skin away from the duck legs and discard it. Pull the meat from the bones, shredding it with a fork or gently with a knife.

3. Just prior to serving, put the greens in a large bowl for tossing. Sauté the mushrooms in the duck fat in a heavy-bottomed skillet until they are browned and fragrant. Add the duck confit and remove from heat. Stir to combine; immediately pour over the salad greens, tossing them to combine.

4. In the still-hot skillet, add the olive oil and lemon juice. Whisk to combine, scraping up any bits from the bottom of the pan. Drizzle over the salad and toss again.

5. Taste before serving; add salt and pepper to taste, and you may wish to add a bit more lemon juice.

Gregg Wershoven (right) with Josh

Mountaintop Mushroom Bean & Clam Stew

SERVES 4

1 cup dried Great Northern beans, rinsed and soaked
for 3 hours
1 pound fresh mushrooms, sliced into 1-inch pieces
2 tablespoons butter
4 large artichokes, trimmed and cooked
2 pounds littleneck clams, rinsed and scrubbed
½ cup plus 2 tablespoons cup dry white wine
½ cup heavy cream
2 tablespoons unsalted butter
1 tablespoon minced parsley
Sea salt and pepper to taste

1. Cook beans in 6 quarts water in a covered pot until completely soft, about 1 hour. Strain into a colander, reserving the bean cooking liquid.

2. Sauté the mushrooms in 2 tablespoons butter until browned. Set aside.

3. Cut the artichoke bottoms into 6 wedges. Stir into the cooked mushrooms, coating them with butter.

4. In a 4-quart pot, steam the clams in ½ cup white wine until they open. Scoop out the clams and their liquid into a clean pot. Discard the white wine.

5. To the clams add the mushrooms, artichokes, drained beans, and cream. Cover and slowly bring the ingredients to a simmer over medium heat. Stir in the butter, parsley, and 2 tablespoons white wine. Season to taste with sea salt and pepper. Serve immediately.

TREAT FARM

361 Old Tavern Rd., Orange, CT 06477 | (203) 799-2453 | www.treatfarm.com

Jeff Wilson is a tall and lanky lad who claims he's an engineer in his "real" life. After a lighthearted chuckle, and hoping I don't tell his boss, Jeff recants and says he's probably just a full-time engineer on the side.

Jeff Wilson

This farm has been in the Treat family for generations, pioneered by Charles and Addie. But it is the brother-sisters trio of Jeff Wilson and his family, Heather Bucknam and her family, and Shelby Wilson that have tripped, quite accidentally, back into farming. Jeff, Heather, and Shelby left the farm to go to college at the urging of their parents, who believed that education would help them build a better life for themselves. Then they inherited this former dairy farm from their parents. For the past sixteen years, they have boldly taken up the farming mantle, creating a successful vegetable and cut-your-own Christmas tree farm.

Their farm is smack dab in a residential area, right off the main drag of Post Road in Orange, Connecticut. In fact, following GPS directions past strip malls, parking lots, and apartment buildings, you'd start to wonder if you're being led on a wild goose chase.

A stunning ninety-acre agricultural oasis, Treat Farm is the very last piece of undeveloped land in this part of town. This unique location allows Jeff, Heather, and Shelby to interact with an urbanite population who would otherwise not have direct access to locally produced foods.

Treat Farm sports some very impressive barns that would make even the architecturally disinterested stand up and take notice. In the late 1800s, one of the barns on the property burned to the ground, killing the dairy

TREAT FARM

361 Old Tavern Road

CONNECTICUT GROWN
THE LOCAL FLAVOR.

THE FRESHEST
PRODUCTS
AVAILABLE!

CATTLE PASS
500 FEET AHEAD
DAIRY FEEDS BB POULTRY FEEDS

ORANGE OPEN FARMS
DAY IS SAT 8/28!

TREAT FARM

HOURS:
MON-FRI 1-6 PM
SAT-SUN 10-6 PM

SWEET CORN
50¢/EAR OR $6.00/DOZ
TOMATOES $2.00/LB
PEPPERS $1.50/LB
EGGPLANT $1.50/LB
GREEN BEANS $1.80/LB
SQUASH $1.00/LB
CUT FLOWERS $5.00/BUNCH
CHERRY/GRAPE TOMATOES $3.50/LB

CUCUMBERS 60¢ EA
PICKLING CUKES $1.50/LB
PEACHES $1.80/LB   GARLIC 15¢
ONIONS $1.20/LB RED ONIONS $1.75/LB
POTATOES $1.20/LB RED POTATOES $1.50/LB
BASIL $2.00/BUNCH
VIDALIAS $1.75/LB
NECTARINES $2.00/LB

ORANGE COUNTRY FAIR

ORANGE COUNTRY FAIR

cattle inside. So unsettling was this loss of livestock in such a heinous manner that the barn rebuilt in its place rests on a first floor made entirely of stone. Should the barn again catch fire, it is designed to keep the animals safe, surrounded by the first-floor vault of stone and concrete, even if the barn burns entirely to the ground. This gigantic red barn, more than three stories tall, stands like a monolith against the rising morning sun.

Jeff loves to travel, and when the farm is sleeping for the winter, this vacation junkie packs up his family and heads for the hills. Traveling to the far corners of distant countries allows Jeff, a self-professed "regular schmuck," and his wife, Carrie, the opportunity to catch some well-deserved rest and relaxation.

Jeff and his sisters are desperately trying to keep the Treat Farm operational. All working full-time in their trained professions, they toil incessantly—learning as they go—to both preserve the legacy of their family as farmers and preserve Treat Farm to pass along to their own children. That is a very heavy burden to carry—straddling two generations as sole stewards of this last piece of undeveloped property in the area.

Treat Farm Greek Fennel Salad

SERVES 4

  2 medium fennel bulbs
  ¾ cup dry white wine
  1 teaspoon honey
  ¼ cup extra virgin olive oil
  1 large shallot, minced

1 heaping teaspoon coriander seeds
Sea salt and freshly ground pepper to taste

1. Cut off a few fronds at the top of the fennel, chop coarsely, and reserve. Cut off the stalks where they join the bulbs. Peel the outer fibers from the fennel bulbs with a vegetable peeler, and cut away any dark patches with a paring knife.

2. Cut the fennel bulbs in half lengthwise. Cut each half into 4 wedges, with a section of core forming the point of the wedge.

3. Arrange the fennel wedges in a single layer in a 6-quart, wide, nonaluminum stockpot. Add the wine, honey, and olive oil, and sprinkle in the shallot and coriander seeds. Bring to a gentle simmer; cover the pot and cook over low heat for about 25 minutes, or until a fork penetrates easily into the fennel but meets slight resistance. Check after 15 minutes.

4. When the fennel is done, remove the lid from the stockpot. If there is more than ½ cup cooking liquid remaining, quickly boil it down to equal ½ cup. Sprinkle the cooked fennel with salt and pepper; sprinkle on the chopped fronds.

5. Serve the wedges hot on individual plates, spooning a few tablespoons of cooking liquid over each. Or serve cold as a salad.

Farmer Jeff's New England Beef Brisket from Scratch

SERVES 8

½ cup kosher salt

1 tablespoon black peppercorns, cracked

¾ teaspoon ground allspice

3 tablespoons fresh thyme

½ tablespoon paprika

2 bay leaves, crumbled

1 fresh beef brisket, about 4–6 pounds

2 pounds carrots, peeled and cut into ½ x 3-inch sticks

2 pounds turnips, peeled and quartered

2 pounds parsnips, peeled and cut into ½ x 3-inch sticks

2 pounds brussels sprouts, whole with stems trimmed

1. Mix the salt and seasonings in a small bowl. Stab the brisket about 30 times per side with a meat fork. Rub each side evenly with the salt-and-spice mixture. Place in a 2-gallon zipper-lock plastic bag, and force as much air out as possible. Place between two rimmed baking sheets and weigh down with two bricks or heavy cans. Refrigerate for 5 to 7 days, turning daily.

2. To prepare brisket for cooking, rinse the meat and pat dry. Bring the brisket to a boil in a large stockpot with just enough water to cover by ½ inch. Skim away impurities that rise to the surface. Cover and simmer until a skewer inserted in the thickest part of the meat slides out with ease, about 2 to 3 hours.

3. Heat oven to 200°F. Transfer the meat to a large oven-proof platter, and spoon 1 cup of the cooking liquid on top; tent with aluminum foil and place in oven.

4. Add carrots and turnips to the cooking liquid and bring to a boil. Cover and simmer until the vegetables just begin to soften, 5 to 10 minutes. Add parsnips and brussels sprouts. Cover and simmer an additional 5 to 10 minutes longer, until all the vegetables are tender.

5. Remove brisket from the oven, and cut it across the grain into ¼-inch slices. Return meat to the platter. Transfer vegetables to the platter; moisten with ½ cup cooking liquid and serve.

Note: There are a total of 8 pounds of vegetables in this recipe. Feel free to use any combination of carrots, rutabagas, turnips, red potatoes, boiling onions, wedged green cabbage, parsnips, or brussels sprouts.

Chapter 6

NEW LONDON COUNTY

❧

Cato Corner Farm

178 Cato Corner Rd., Colchester, CT 06415 | (860) 537-3884 | www.catocornerfarm.com

Elizabeth and Mark McAlister are anything but your typical dairy farmers. This mother-son team also offers grass-fed beef and veal from their rotational forty-acre pasture-based dairy operation, known throughout Connecticut as Cato Corner Farm.

Mark is the cheese maestro. A former school teacher in Baltimore, this bright young Irish descendant returned to Connecticut to take up the challenge of creating aged and edible, simply divine confections with milk.

With nearly 3,000 gallons of milk produced every one to two days, Cato Corner Farm is a cheese-making machine, churning out over 400 pounds of cheese that is sent directly down into the cheese cave for ripening, finishing, and fruiting. Mark creates all-natural rind cheeses, all from his own inventive recipes. The cave contains cheeses made both yesterday and more than a year ago displayed on what appears to be a bookshelf from my first apartment. I recognized the board-and-cinder-block arrangement immediately. Such fond memories!

Liz is a feisty and politically oriented dynamo, almost always flanked by her two attentive border collies, in the traditional dress of overalls, a blue bandana, and Tevas. Liz has been at Cato Corner Farm since 1979, previously having been a commercial sheep and goat farmer. She prefers dairy cows, feeling that these animals are her calling. She now has an opportunity to interact with her animals on a personal level.

Liz grew up in Rhode Island, where her father was a doctor, and I'm quite sure there were expectations of high society and white picket fences. With a throwback nod to the Back to the Land movement of the 1960s, this extraordinarily independent woman finds great satisfaction in a job that allows her to be involved in the production of something from the beginning to the end. "There's not a lot of things in our culture that allow you to do that."

Elizabeth is extremely shy in speaking about herself. It's not terribly pertinent as far as she's concerned. Although she's an avid reader and finds great solace in poetry, Liz finds it more necessary to remind us of the people who produce our local food, what they're doing with their farms, and how they're going to survive. We always need to talk about the fact that, in her words, "there ain't much farmland left. We just haven't come to grips with the fact that if we don't get our backsides in gear to preserve our land—it's more than just a passing fad of what we'd like to eat—we're going to lose it. All of it." Preservation is more than a fun activity for this activist, for it is the dedicated Connecticut Farmland Trust that allows Cato Corner Farm to exist today.

CATO
CORNER
FARM

FARMSTEAD CHEESE

SAT 10-3
SUN 10-3

CHEESE

Mark McAlister

Liz McAlister

To say that Cato Corner Farm is famous for their cheeses is an understatement of epic proportions. So is the notion that Liz McAlister is just another meek and mild dairy farmer. I'll continue to cheer her on.

Elizabeth's Irish Onion Soup

SERVES 4

4 tablespoons butter
6 medium onions, sliced thin
1 teaspoon sea salt
1 tablespoon fresh thyme leaves
½ teaspoon allspice
1 bay leaf
¼ cup apple cider vinegar

1½ cups Guinness, or other dark beer
5 cups low-sodium chicken broth
Sea salt and pepper to taste
6 slices country bread, cut ½-inch thick and toasted
1 clove garlic, halved
½ pound Cato Corner Bridgid's Abbey, Bloomsday, or Dutch Farmstead cheese

1. Melt butter in an 8-quart soup kettle over medium heat. Add the sliced onions and sea salt, and stir to coat the onions in butter.

2. Cook over low to medium heat, stirring frequently, until onions are reduced, browned, and syrupy and

the inside of the pan is coated with a brown crust. (Patience is the key, and the slower the better!)

3. Add the thyme, allspice, bay leaf, vinegar, and beer. Simmer until the beer is reduced by half, about 20 minutes. Add the chicken stock, scraping the pot to loosen the browned bits. Simmer on low for another 20 minutes. Discard the bay leaf; season with sea salt and pepper.

4. To serve: Adjust the oven rack to the upper middle position and preheat the broiler. Set serving bowls on a baking sheet and fill ⅔ full with soup. Top with bread toasts that have been rubbed with the cut end of raw garlic and topped with equal slices of cheese.

5. Broil until well browned and bubbly, about 10 minutes. Allow to cool for 5 minutes before serving.

Cato Corner Farm
Blue Cheese Roasted Brussels Sprouts
SERVES 4
  2 pounds brussels sprouts
  3 tablespoons butter, melted
  ¾ teaspoon sea salt
  1½ teaspoons pepper
  ¼ cup crumbled Cato Corner Hooligan
     or other blue cheese

1. Preheat the oven to 400°F. Cut off the brown ends of the brussels sprouts and pull off any yellow outer leaves. Mix them in a bowl with melted butter, sea salt, and pepper.

2. Roast in a single layer in a 13-quart casserole dish for about 35–40 minutes, until crisp on the outside and tender on the inside. Stir often to brown evenly.

3. Remove from oven and sprinkle with crumbled cheese. Allow to rest for 5 minutes before serving to allow the cheese to melt. Serve warm.

CEDAR MEADOW FARM

12 Erins Way, Ledyard, CT 06339 | (860) 608-7442 | www.cedarmeadowfarm.net

Peter Cronin is the reason Cedar Meadow Farm exists today. At age ten, and with extreme health issues that continue to require surgeries, he is a lively and active preteen who uses his bicycle as his main form of transportation. It was his diagnosis of severe food allergies that brought his parents, Brian and Julia, two highly trained chemists, out of the workforce and into the dirt to produce their own food. Deathly allergic to commercially produced dairy, soy, and eggs, Peter now participates in the family farm, eating to his heart's content all of food that he helps raise—free of chemicals and commercial additives—foods that were once restricted from his diet.

With land so expensive in Connecticut, the Cronins sold their four-bedroom house, purchased a wooded lot, erected a 760-square-foot yurt, and spent the next eighteen months living with their three children under one tent without electricity, plumbing, or running water as they cleared their land by hand and built their new house. And, yes, they're still happily married—despite the small cabinet obscuring the compostable toilet.

Julia and Brian are the only farmers I've met who didn't inherit a farm or buy an existing farming property with already cleared pasture lands and some sort of prebuilt infrastructure. This brilliant and amicable couple built a farm purely from scratch. Because they did, it is one of the more unusual places that I've visited, with the yurt still standing and functioning as the family's barn.

Every animal at Cedar Meadow Farm is here for a reason. Using animals to clear the land, Julia and Brian have created a symbiotic partnership between these creatures and the land, between these creatures and the very fabric of their family. The ram was sent out first to clear the thistle and invasive exotics and poisonous plants; followed by the pigs, which helped dig the roots and overturn rocks; then the chickens; then the sheep and horses to continue to graze down the native grasses.

Jack the Ass is the guard donkey. Since donkeys hate canines, he protects the sheep from coyotes. When Ben, the Scottish blackface ram, isn't hanging out with his best friend, Reed the horse, you'll find him with Jack the Ass, playing together in their various romparound, made-up games-du-jour. They're all together, not separated by beams or electric wires.

There is a feeling of magic at Cedar Meadow Farm. Visiting the Cronins puts one in direct contact with all of these animals, since their Garden of Eden has minimal fencing and electric barbs that ensure an impersonal "look, but don't touch" atmosphere. Walking around is an invitation for curious sheep to rub against your legs like cats in search of attention or for the sows within arm's reach to grunt a bit in acknowledgment of your presence. Ben and Jack are the friendliest, although Ben's horns are a bit unnerving at first, being rather large, pointy, and in direct line with one's kneecaps. I wasn't quite prepared. I was terribly nervous at first to have a 300-pound ram resting against my legs in a gesture of welcome. Then I really liked it.

Emme and Peter Cronin

Peter Cronin

Peter's Curried Egg Salad

SERVES 4

6 large eggs
½ cup whole-milk yogurt
¼ cup dried apricots, diced small
2 teaspoons curry powder
2 teaspoons apple cider
¼ cup minced fresh spinach
Sea salt and pepper to taste

1. Place eggs in a 4-quart saucepan; cover with 1 inch of water, and bring to a boil over high heat. Remove pan from heat, cover, and let sit for 10 minutes. Place pan in the sink and flood with cold running water for about 5 minutes, or transfer eggs to a bowl filled with water and ice cubes. When eggs are cool, peel and dice.

2. In a separate bowl, combine all other ingredients. Add eggs, and mix to combine. Cover and refrigerate for at least 1 hour, until the flavors meld and the apricots soften.

Julia, Emme, and Brian Cronin

Cedar Meadow Farm
Slow Roasted Fresh Ham

SERVES 6–8

1 bone-in fresh ham with skin, about 6–8 pounds
2 cups Arlow's Beer Maple Glaze (See page 56.)

Brine

3 cups kosher salt or 1½ cups table salt
2 heads garlic
10 bay leaves
⅓ cup black peppercorns

Herb paste

½ cup lightly packed sage leaves
½ cup parsley leaves
1 garlic clove
1 teaspoon sea salt
½ teaspoon pepper
¼ cup extra virgin olive oil

1. For the ham and brine: Carefully slice through the skin and fat with a serrated knife, making a 1-inch diamond pattern. Be careful not to cut into the meat.

2. In a large bucket or stockpot, dissolve the salt in 4 quarts water. Add the garlic, bay leaves, and peppercorns. Submerge the ham in the brine and refrigerate 8 to 24 hours.

3. Set a large disposable roasting pan on a baking sheet, and place a flat wire rack in the pan. Remove the ham from the brine; rinse under cold water and dry thoroughly with paper towels. Place the ham cut side down and skin side up on the wire rack. Let stand at room temperature for 1 hour. Adjust the oven rack to the lowest position and heat the oven to 500°F.

4. Puree sage, parsley, garlic, sea salt, pepper, and olive oil in a food processor until the mixture forms a smooth paste. Rub over all sides of the ham.

5. Roast the ham at 500°F for 20 minutes. Reduce the oven temperature to 350°F and continue to roast, brushing the ham with glaze every 30 to 45 minutes, until the center of the ham registers 145°F, about 2½ hours.

6. Remove ham from oven and tent loosely with foil. Allow to rest at room temperature for at least 20 to 30 minutes, until the ham registers 155°F on a meat thermometer. Carve and serve.

DAVIS FARM

568 Greenhaven Rd., Pawcatuck, CT 06379 | Dara Karas: (860) 599-2810

John Whitman Davis, better known as "Whit," is by far one of Connecticut's most celebrated farmers and one of our most cherished elders. Located in the Pawcatuck area of Stonington, the Davis Farm has been farmed since 1632. An eighty-six-year-old who just moved out of his original homestead, devoid of running water and electricity, a mere nineteen years ago, Whit started farming at the age of eleven. He hasn't stopped since. Whit is the eleventh generation of farmers in his family, and his son Larry is the twelfth. Perhaps a great-grandson will become the thirteenth.

The original homestead, now preserved as the Stanton-Davis Homestead Museum, maintains the artifacts, etchings, drawings, and pictorial family stories of the African slaves who worked the land for former Davis Family generations. Standing tributes to these slaves remain throughout the farm, a reminder of our pre–Civil War history and of Whit's deep morality in

Stanton-Davis Homestead Museum

Whit Davis

you'll find a flavor and taste that is dense and chocolaty, reminding me less of the watery and crunchy-sweet crisp of the genetically modified sweet corn we serve at our tables today and more like a creamy fire-roasted butternut squash left to cook buried beneath the campfire embers. In the 1940s research indicated that this corn has been grown for more than a thousand years by the American Indians who traveled northward and eastward from the Maya. Only three growers remain: two in Rhode Island and Whit Davis.

Davis's farm is not in the business of agriculture per se. Whit is in the business of preserving land and history and doing his one small part to right the historical wrongs of our society. His tool? Corn.

The Native American tribes in Connecticut have lost their traditional planting grounds due to, as Whit says, "the white man's greed." In the 1920s the State of Connecticut took more than one hundred acres of the Mohegan's land near Fort Shantok, waited until the tribe received federal recognition, and then sold it back to them for over a million dollars.

"Now that isn't right," says Whit. "I'm in the Indians' corner." And he is. Whit works fourteen-hour days and arrives each year at the hearth of the region's remaining tribes with baskets of native food—not unlike the scenes of Native Americans providing the *Mayflower* passengers with food for our first Thanksgiving. "I'm returning it back," he says. And he does, returning ancestral seed and corn to tribes up and down the East Coast.

acknowledging the past and paying tribute to the hardworking individuals upon whose backs the Davis Farm was built to survive these hundreds of years later.

Whit's famous Johnny Cake corn variety, a descendant of the Native American corn, or maize, has been farmed on Davis land since 1634 without missing a crop. You've never seen corn like this. Ever. The cobs are longer by nearly four inches and narrower by nearly two. You can eat this native corn only in the milk stage without first drying and grinding it. When you do,

Without working capital, with finances stretched to the limit, a shortage of farm workers, and the creaking bones of a body in its eighty-sixth year, Whit retrains Native American cultures in how to grow and harvest their traditional seeds, their ancestral foods.

Whit Davis is the Godfather of Connecticut. "You people had better realize that once it's gone, it's gone!" he sighs. "They're not making any more land. If you want to keep developing it for condominiums and fancy houses, you won't have it to survive on. It will be destroyed!"

We had better realize that about Whit too. Find the man who always carries a cob of corn in his pocket. You have much to learn—and perhaps not a lot of time to learn it.

A tribute to African-American slaves

Whit Davis's Famous Johnny Cakes

Davis family recipe, used with permission.

SERVES 4

> 1 cup white corn meal
> ½ teaspoon sea salt
> About 2 cups boiling water
> A little milk
> A little sugar, if desired

1. Combine corn meal and sea salt in a bowl. Add enough boiling water to reach the consistency of oatmeal. Add a little milk to thin a bit and a little sugar to taste.

2. Drop by teaspoonfuls on a hot griddle that has been greased with corn oil. Cook 5 or 6 minutes, turning once, until golden brown. Keep skillet well-greased with corn oil.

Note: Sometimes Whit puts the entire cornmeal mixture into a greased 9-inch casserole. Bake at 350°F for 30–40 minutes until a toothpick inserted into the center comes out dry. To serve, cut it into wedges like pie.

Davis Farm Corn Bread Muffins

MAKES 12 MUFFINS

> 2 cups white cornmeal
> 3 cups flour
> 3 tablespoons baking powder
> 1½ teaspoons sea salt
> ¼ cup packed dark brown sugar
> 3 tablespoons honey
> 3 eggs, beaten
> 2 cups milk
> ½ cup butter, melted

1. Preheat oven to 400°F. Whisk the cornmeal, flour, baking powder, sea salt, and brown sugar together in a large bowl. In a separate bowl, combine honey, eggs, and milk. Add the wet and dry ingredients together until just barely combined. Drizzle melted butter over the batter, and stir until the ingredients are just combined.

2. Pour the batter into butter-greased muffin tins or cupcake liners. Bake at 400°F until the muffins are golden brown and lightly cracked around the edges, 20 to 25 minutes. Transfer to a wire rack to cool. Serve drizzled with honey, with a bit of butter, or just plain.

SOELTL FARM

395 Forsyth Rd., Salem, CT 06420 | (860) 887-3329 | www.soeltlfarm.com

Soeltl Farm is, as Donna Lesczczynski puts it, "just a wee scosche of a place," and she views it more as a family-run homestead than a large operational farm. Complete with a wild parrot in the kitchen that bites, this farm is totally self sufficient. Donna and her family spend hours in the vegetable garden, canning, preserving, and creating all their own food.

A retired construction worker severely injured on the job, Donna, with her waist-length hair and round glasses, is unpretentious and modest. This clever intellectual is bighearted and generous, quick to share the fruits of her labor from the family's own pantry. We first met on Facebook, and she also finds a few moments at the start of every day to participate in one of my secret and guilty pleasures, *Mafia Wars.*

The Lesczczynski family started farming just to produce food for themselves. The demand for locally produced food from neighbors encouraged them to expand their operation. And, yes, the word has spread about these purveyors of epicurean livestock.

In addition to duck, goose, turkey, and chicken eggs and home-spun honey, the Soeltl Farm produces veal, beef, pigs, goats, geese, turkeys, chickens, ducks, and Cornish cross chickens—all without growth hormones, stimulants, or constant antibiotic use. They have a dairy herd but don't sell their milk, since their animals are all milk-fed—one of the secrets to why their products are so flavorful. And being one of the very few producers of fowl in Connecticut, Soeltl Farm is exploring the creation of a USDA-inspected poultry slaughter area on-site—a desperately needed addition to our state's agricultural economy.

This family is perfectly at ease in their work boots and in their own skin. Following Donna around on the farm means interrupted human conversations to ensure proper greeting of each animal in the pasture by name,

Nan Lesczczynski

with all the appropriate scratches, nuzzles, and ear rubs.

Donna loves working in agriculture and loves watching her two young children growing up on a farm. It's clear that her children are having a wonderful time. Nan tends the chicks like a mother and is learning to ride the horses, while Donna's teenage son has a wild-eyed look of concentration as he studies how to maneuver the gigantic farm machinery. With a matter-of-fact gaze, Donna says, "Anyone can do this. If you have the opportunity, you should."

Donna's Duck Confit

SERVES 4–10

2 ducks
2 teaspoons sea salt
2 teaspoons freshly ground black pepper
3 cloves garlic, minced
1½ tablespoons fresh thyme
3 cloves

1. Remove the legs from the two ducks, setting them aside in a bowl. Save the duck breasts for another meal. Leave the skin attached to the legs, but remove any excess. In a separate bowl, trim all the excess fat off the duck (except that covering the breasts reserved for a separate meal).

2. Mash the salt, pepper, garlic, and thyme in a mortar and pestle. Rub mixture into the duck legs. Cover them with plastic wrap and allow to marinate for at least 1 hour.

3. To render duck fat: Chop the duck fat in a food processor. Put the chopped fat in a 4-quart, heavy-bottomed pot over low to medium heat. Cook, stirring often and not allowing the fat to get too hot, until the fat runs clear. Depending on the amount of fat, this may take 20 minutes or 2 hours. Carefully strain the fat. Use it immediately to make confit, or store in the refrigerator up to 6 months.

4. To make the confit: Add the 3 cloves garlic to the rendered duck fat in a 1-quart heavy-bottomed pot and warm gently. Nestle the duck legs, skin side down, into the fat. Starting with low heat, adjust the temperature minimally to ensure that the surface of the confit is gently boiling. Cook for about 1½ to 3 hours until the fat again runs clear and a knife stuck into one of the legs slides in and out easily.

5. Using tongs, remove the duck legs and place in a container just large enough to hold them closely. Strain the fat from the pan over the duck legs. (To store in the refrigerator, make sure the meat is completely covered with fat and no pieces of meat are breaking through the surface.)

6. Serve whole confit legs as a main course, in Gregg's Mushroom & Duck Confit Salad (See page 128.), or as an accompaniment to steamed spinach, Swiss chard, cabbage, or beans. To use as an accompaniment, pull the skin away from the duck legs and discard it. Pull the meat off the bones and shred it with a fork or gently with a knife.

Note: Since duck confit is so flavorful, a little goes a very long way.

Soeltl Farm Chicken Liver Mousse

SERVES 4

10 ounces chicken livers, cleaned of blood vessels
   and fat
1 teaspoon sea salt
1 teaspoon pepper
2 tablespoons extra virgin olive oil
2 shallots, chopped fine
1 clove garlic, chopped fine
1 teaspoon fresh thyme
⅛ teaspoon nutmeg
¼ cup port, Madeira, or dry cream sherry
½ pound unsalted butter, slightly colder than room
   temperature
1 cup heavy cream, cold
Sea salt and pepper to taste

1. Rinse and drain the livers and pat them dry.
   Sprinkle livers with sea salt and pepper, and sauté
   in a single layer in oil over very high heat. Brown
   the livers for 1 to 3 minutes on each side, or until
   they feel slightly firm to the touch. Using a slotted
   spoon, transfer the livers to a food processor.

2. Discard the oil from the sauté pan and, while it
   is still hot, add the shallots, garlic, thyme, and
   nutmeg. Stir until fragrant, about 30 seconds.

3. Remove pan from heat and add the alcohol.
   Return pan to heat; bring alcohol to a boil and
   reduce it to about half. Pour the hot alcohol
   mixture over the livers; allow to cool for about 10
   minutes.

4. Puree the livers in the food processor, adding the
   butter in pieces while the blade is turning. Transfer
   the liver pâté to a bowl and season to taste with
   sea salt and pepper. Allow the pâté to cool to room
   temperature.

5. Whip the cream to medium peaks and quickly
   whisk ¼ of the cream into the liver pâté. Gently
   fold the remaining cream into the pâté to create
   a mousse. Store with plastic wrap pressing down
   against the surface of the mousse to prevent it from
   coming into contact with the air. Chill the mousse
   for at least 3 hours or overnight.

6. Serve with dense, crusty bread and something
   pickled.

STONINGTON SEAFOOD HARVESTERS

4 High St., Stonington, CT 06378 | (860) 535-8342

The brawny Bomster brothers can completely fill a room with their booming voices, adventurous spirits, and amusing stories. Scallop fishing employs the entire Bomster family. Melayna, Billy's wife, is the accountant, and the other brothers, Mike and Joe, are both captains. They're training the younger family members to take over the business, since the career of a fisherman starts drawing to a close in his or her mid-fifties.

The first boat Joe and Billy purchased together to join their father in the family business was the *Duchess*. It sank on a dark and stormy night about forty miles south of Martha's Vineyard. Four members of the Bomster family, rescued by an offshore lobster boat in the dead stillness of an October night, watched the boys' first investment roll over and sink.

I thought the story was significant—most people might give pause at the thought of nearly drowning in the middle of the ocean at 2:00 a.m.—but Billy threw his hands in the air. "Listen, this wasn't like the *Titanic* going down with people flippin' out and jumpin' over the side! It was all pretty organized." He's like that—steadfast, in an understated, pokerfaced sort of way.

The Brothers Bomster built the *Patty Jo* in 1988 and bought the *Stonington Jo* out of Alaska in 2001.

Each boat fishes sixty-five days a year, mandated by government restrictions to save and preserve the scallop population. As for scallop fishing in general, there has been a moratorium on permits since 1989. The only way to fish for scallops is to purchase an existing scallop permit, which is tied to particular boats and nontransferable. That means one has to buy both a scallop permit and the $5 million boat the permit is attached to before heading out to sea in search of these edible bivalves.

In a case of unbelievable luck, the Bomster boys found a scallop boat in Alaska with an East Coast permit. The *Stonington Jo* made the long trip down the West Coast, through the Panama Canal, and up to Virginia, where the Bomsters picked her up and brought her to her current berth at the Stonington docks.

During downtime on the docks, the Bomster family has built a fantastic little business on High Street. There is a walk-in store, complete with freezers and a credit card machine—a serve-yourself plethora of scallops and seafood of all kinds, including salmon, shrimp, flounder, crab cakes, and much more provided by friends of the family and other qualified fishermen. The Bomster brothers know their fish. The quality is unparalleled. "We don't sell crap just to save a dollar!" Billy roars. And they don't.

Joe and Billy Bomster

Bomster's Bay Scallops with Smoked Salmon Sauce

SERVES 4

    8 large bay scallops
    Sea salt and pepper
    4 tablespoons butter
    2 teaspoons balsamic vinegar
    1 ounce smoked salmon, shredded
    1 teaspoon finely chopped fresh chives

1. Generously salt and pepper the bay scallops. Sauté scallops in butter, turning often, until browned and cooked through. Remove scallops to a platter.

2. In a separate bowl, combine balsamic vinegar, salmon, and chives. Add to the hot pan and cook, whisking vigorously to loosen browned bits, about 20 seconds. Immediately pour over scallops and serve.

Stonington Joe's Scallop Newburg

SERVES 4

3 pounds small bay scallops

4 tablespoons butter, divided

4 tablespoons minced shallots

½ cup shredded parsnips

½ cup shredded apples

½ cup shredded carrots

2 cloves garlic, minced

4 tablespoons brandy

4 tablespoons freshly squeezed orange juice, divided

½ cup clam juice

1 cup heavy cream

¼ teaspoon nutmeg

¼ teaspoon cayenne pepper

½ teaspoon sea salt

½ teaspoon pepper

4 large egg yolks

2 tablespoons minced parsley

2 teaspoons minced tarragon

Sea salt and pepper to taste

1. In a heavy-bottomed 14-inch skillet, sauté scallops in 2 tablespoons butter until lightly browned on both sides. Transfer to a bowl. Add remaining 2 tablespoons butter and sauté shallots, parsnips, apples, and carrots until softened, about 8 minutes. Add garlic and sauté until fragrant, about 30 seconds. Add brandy, 3 tablespoons orange juice, and clam juice; bring to a simmer. Simmer, stirring occasionally until the sauce has reduced to about ¾ cup, about 5 minutes.

2. With an emersion blender, puree the stock to a smooth consistency. Add the cream, nutmeg, cayenne, sea salt, and pepper. Cook until the sauce has thickened slightly and reduced to 1½ cups. Turn the heat down low.

3. Whisk egg yolks in a large bowl. Slowly stir ½ cup of the hot cream mixture into the yolks. Slowly add the tempered egg mixture back into the simmering cream mixture, stirring constantly until the sauce and egg have combined.

4. Add the scallops, parsley, tarragon, and remaining 1 tablespoon orange juice. Season to taste with sea salt and pepper. Serve immediately over rice, puff pastry, or toast crisps.

Chapter 7

TOLLAND COUNTY

BUSH MEADOW FARM

738 Buckley Hwy., Union, CT 06076 | (860) 684-3089 | www.bushmeadowfarm.com

Nancy Kapplan calls her operation a "Country Dining Place"—reminiscent of Mayberry, a place where people come, hang out, and chat with their neighbors. At the rising light of dawn, the Bush Meadow Farm store and cafe quickly fills with locals, neighbors, policemen, and cyclists here for good food—fresh food—both tended in the fields and prepared in the kitchen by the Kapplan family.

Most of the wares served at the Bush Meadow Farm Country Dining Place are made directly from or at their farm, including their own handmade cheeses, old-fashioned aged gelato, and Barry's artisanal charcuterie. Barry is the only artisanal *charcutier* in Connecticut, making pastrami, smoked briskets, bacon, Canadian bacon, and much, much more. As if they don't have enough to keep them busy, Barry and Nancy farm thirty-seven acres, with nearly sixty goats, chickens, and a sugarhouse. They'll soon start cultivating mushrooms.

Barry is a retired U.S. Army major, combat disabled in the 1991Gulf War. Stationed over the years at Fort Bliss in El Paso, Texas, where Jacob was born; Fort Meade in Maryland, where the twins were born; Frankfurt, Germany, where the youngest was born; Fort Irwin in California; Fort Rucker in Alabama; and Fort Eustis in Virginia, the Kapplans have taken to the small town of Union, Connecticut, like fish to water.

A native of New Britain, Connecticut, and an ICU nurse at Walter Reed Army Medical Center in Washington, D.C., Nancy absolutely loved the Army life. It was Barry, in need of more space, who quietly requested that the family pack their bags to leave Washington and return to Connecticut. After purchasing the property in 2005 upon which they have since created Bush Meadow Farm, they found through historical research that members of Nancy's family had originally owned pieces of this very land in the 1700s—an epic homecoming in a completely unexpected way.

The entire Kapplan family has participated in our nation's history. Feeling responsible for knowing the history of the land from which they derive their income and feeling obligated as stewards of that land, Nancy and Barry believe that there is more they can do.

Their son Jacob is a combat veteran of Operation Iraq Freedom with the National Guard. He is now an ICU nurse in the transplant unit at Hartford Hospital. David, one of the twins, will finish nursing school in 2011. Twin sister Ariel just started law school and is not terribly pleased to share her name with a Disney character. Taryn, the youngest and the celebrated gelato maker, just graduated as an accounting major and tends to the kitchen at breakfast.

Nancy and Barry are not without a wickedly naughty sense of humor, my favorite kind. While the

Nancy Kapplan

Bush Meadow Farm Bacon Bruschetta

SERVES 4

1 loaf country bread in 1-inch slices, lightly toasted
3 tablespoons extra virgin olive oil
1 large garlic clove, halved

Topping

4 medium yellow summer squash or zucchini, seeded
*   and diced*
1 tablespoon apple cider
1 teaspoon fresh lemon juice
2 tablespoons extra virgin olive oil
½ teaspoon sea salt
½ teaspoon black pepper
4 strips bacon, fried until crisp and minced
4 ounces blue cheese, crumbled
¼ cup shredded fresh spinach

1. Adjust oven rack 4 inches away from the broiler.

2. Brush both sides of toasted bread with olive oil, and rub with the clove of garlic.

3. Combine squash, apple cider, lemon juice, olive oil, sea salt, and pepper in a medium bowl and allow to stand for 5 minutes. Toss in bacon, cheese, and spinach.

4. Divide the mixture evenly among the bread slices. Broil bruschetta until the cheese begins to melt, about 1½ minutes. Serve immediately.

American flag waves proudly by the front door, near the entrance of their delightful cafe and country store is also a rather inconspicuous phallic symbol—a token of their secret thoughts about world affairs or politics or whatever. After a farm-fresh breakfast and stopping to pet the goats, see if you can find it. So very, very funny.

Kapplan Family Goat Cheese Quiche

SERVES 6

½ recipe Farmer Erica's Perfect Piecrust (page 199),
   or 1 refrigerated piecrust
½ cup thinly sliced onions
¼ cup grated apples
2 tablespoons butter
½ cup Canadian bacon, diced small
¼ teaspoon ground nutmeg
½ cup chopped arugula, loosely packed
6 large eggs
⅔ cup heavy cream
½ cup whole milk
6 ounces fresh goat cheese
2 teaspoons sea salt
2 teaspoons pepper

1. Preheat oven to 425°F. Roll out pie dough to fit a
   10½-inch glass pie plate. Crimp the edges, and poke
   the bottom with a fork or tip of a knife. Place in the
   freezer for 10 minutes. Bake piecrust in the bottom
   ⅓ of the oven until pastry is golden, about 15 to 20
   minutes. Remove from the oven and reserve.

2. In a heavy-bottomed skillet, sauté onions and
   apples in butter until browned. Add Canadian
   bacon, nutmeg, and arugula and sauté over low
   to medium heat until the greens are cooked and
   the bacon begins to brown, about 4 or 5 minutes.
   Distribute evenly in the piecrust.

3. In a medium-size bowl, whisk together the eggs,
   cream, milk, and goat cheese until thoroughly
   blended. Season with sea salt and pepper. Pour over
   the Canadian bacon mixture in the pie shell.

4. Reduce the oven temperature to 350°F and bake
   in the center of the oven until the filling is golden
   and puffed and is completely baked through, about
   30 minutes. Serve immediately.

JOHNNY APPLESEED'S FARM

13 Schoolhouse Rd., Ellington, CT 06029 | (860) 875-1030 | www.freewebs.com/johnnyappleseedct

Ken and Kim Shores are the feisty proprietors of Johnny Appleseed's Farm. A cute couple with a propensity toward laughter, they cultivate more than 150 acres of land yielding apples, peaches, plums, sweet corn, pumpkins, tomatoes, winter squash, Christmas trees, and Christmas wreathes.

Their farm was created by a land developer in the 1970s. When the land development business proved unfruitful, he created an apple orchard as a hobby. Thirty years ago, as a strapping young man in search of a job, Kenny worked at the orchard, staying on to become the farm manager and finally purchasing the business in 1989.

In 1984 Kim arrived in Connecticut from Pennsylvania, taking a job at Johnny Appleseed's Farm. She quickly fell in love with her boss, and Kenny and Kim have been happily married ever since. As for concerns about spouses working together all these years, this rosy-cheeked couple just giggle, roll their eyes, and share a look that only married people can give each other. They epitomize the words of the song "Love and Marriage": "They go together like a horse and carriage."

Quick to dispel the myth that farmers don't have much work to do in the wintertime, Kenny and Kim work their fingers to the bone but look forward to brief vacations every January—preferably someplace warm—for just a few days or so, just to get away together.

Kenny observes that people often have a predisposed opinion of farming. "When they come and visit the farm, everything is green and pretty and you're outside in beautiful weather." Kenny sighs. "They think the feeling that they're getting is the feeling *you* have all the time! That you're lazing out in your pickup with a cigar and the wind blowing through your hair."

What visitors don't comprehend is the difficult business operations of agricultural production: managing labor, twenty-hour days, the crunch of a recession, and the struggle not to raise prices at the risk of their personal welfare.

Unlike many other farmers in Connecticut, Kenny and Kim did not inherit their land from farming ancestors, nor do they have a second generation beneath them to pass the farm along to. At Johnny Appleseed's Farm, it is only Ken and Kim. Between the months of April and November, they can never leave the property together. One of the two of them is always around—a massive commitment that is not always understood or appreciated. Buying a locally grown apple means that this two-person food operation has declined a weekend barbecue at the lake with friends or a camping trip or a late-night movie date.

Such is the dedication to producing your food that makes the all-too-brief visit to family over the holidays so very special for Kenny and Kim. When you visit Johnny Appleseed's Farm, you'll see firsthand their pledge and devotion to quality food production. When you meet them, you'll like them instantly. Next time I go, I'll bring Ken a cigar. No doubt he has earned it.

Johnny Appleseed's Farm Appled Pork Tenderloin

SERVES 4

> 1 boneless pork tenderloin, 2–2½ pounds
> 1 teaspoon sea salt
> 1 teaspoon pepper
> 1 tablespoon extra virgin olive oil or lard
> 1 large onion, sliced thin
> 2 bay leaves
> 5 sprigs thyme
> 8 juniper berries (or 2 tablespoons gin)
> 8 allspice berries
> ¾ teaspoon sea salt
> 3 Granny Smith apples, cored and chopped coarsely
> 1 small red cabbage (about 1½ pounds) quartered, cored, sliced ¼ inch thick
> ½ cup apple cider
> 2 tablespoons maple syrup
> 1 tablespoon coarse French mustard
> 2 tablespoons apple cider vinegar
> Sea salt and pepper to taste

1. Preheat oven to 300°F. Season the tenderloin generously with sea salt and pepper. Heat the oil in a large ovenproof Dutch oven over medium heat, and brown the roast thoroughly on all sides. Transfer the roast to a plate.

2. To the hot pot add onion, bay leaves, thyme sprigs, juniper berries, allspice berries, and sea salt. Cook, scraping the browned bits off the bottom of the pan, until the onions are soft and beginning to brown.

3. Add the apples and cabbage, and cook until the cabbage has softened. Stir in the cider and maple syrup. Lay the roast on top of the cabbage. Cover the pot and transfer to the oven. Cook until a meat thermometer placed in the thickest part of the roast registers 130°F, about 45 to 50 minutes.

4. Transfer the roast to a carving board and tent loosely with aluminum foil. Add mustard to the cabbage mixture and cook on the stovetop over medium heat until the excess liquid has evaporated. Add the vinegar, and season with salt and pepper. Remove the bay leaves and thyme. You may also remove the allspice and juniper berries.

5. Slice the pork into ½-inch-thick rounds. Serve immediately with the apples and cabbage.

Kenny & Kim's Apple Soup

SERVES 4

4 thick slices bacon, cut into ¼-inch cubes

1 large red onion, sliced thin

3 parsnips, peeled and diced

3½ cups low-sodium chicken broth

½ cup apple cider

3 large tart apples, cored and diced

1 medium red potato, diced

¼ teaspoon ground cloves

½ cup whole-milk yogurt

Sea salt and pepper to taste

1. In a 4-quart saucepan, cook bacon until browned and crisped. Remove bacon and set aside. In the same pot, sauté the onion in the remaining bacon fat until just beginning to brown. Add parsnips and cook until browned on all sides and just beginning to caramelize.

2. Add chicken broth, apple cider, apples, potatoes, and ground cloves. Simmer until the potatoes can be pierced with a fork. Puree the soup in a blender or with an immersion blender until smooth and creamy. Add yogurt and bring to a simmer. Add sea salt and pepper to taste.

3. Serve in warmed bowls garnished with bacon.

Kenny and Kim Shores

MILLIX FAMILY FARM

276 Village Hill Rd., Willington, CT 06279 | (860) 684-1313 | www.millixfamilyfarm.com

Millix Family Farm does not instantly fit the mental imagery of an agricultural operation. Located on just three acres in suburban Willington, Patricia Millix tends more than seventy chickens, a garden, five kids, a dog named Ruby, a pony, and a bakery.

Although Patricia is not quite able to do as much farming as she would like in this residential neighborhood, and struggling with the affordability of farmland and finding commercial kitchens, this blond and beautiful super mom has made a successful agricultural life for herself—farming and cooking, using local ingredients within the paradigm of limitations. She dreams of cows, goats, leasing land, and perhaps building a storefront.

Patricia grew up on a farm, and she's passing down that legacy to her children, who help her in the bakery and with the chickens. In the meantime, the Millix Family Farm Bakery is famous for its award-winning apple pie, scones, cookies, breads, cakes, custards, and prepared meals. And of course she has eggs.

The other half of the Millix empire, Tyler, is the busy manager of Tolland County's 911 dispatch center, the fire chief, and a selectman. Son Riley, at fourteen, wants to be an architect. Ten-year-old Molly is avidly planning for her dreams of a huge ranch overflowing with horses, wanting nothing more than a little car and a gigantic truck. Eight-year-old Anna has resolutely decided that she'll take over the bakery when she has finished growing and dreams of creating a colossal store where only local products are available for sale. Emma, six, wants the California glamour life, with a glassy house on the beach and chickens. Yes, chickens. And while the youngest tot is in the throes of the Terrible Twos and hasn't quite decided what he wants to do, it is evident that Patricia has passed along a love of tending land, growing food, and her own philosophy that the most important thing that we can do is engage directly with what we eat.

It was with wide-eyed wonder and an involuntary roar of laughter that I witnessed the chickens being released from their clean and roomy outdoor coop at about 1:00 p.m. And then? They run. More than seventy chickens run like hell in an autobahn race for the clover, free to roam throughout this suburban neighborhood—an unfenced maze of neighborhood backyards, green grass, manicured hedges, swept porches, and swimming pools. It's a sight to see! A sight that is excruciatingly beautiful in its simplicity. Patricia reminds us that the littlest things are extraordinary, and possible.

Patricia's Egg & Butter Pound Cake

SERVES 8

    1 cup butter, room temperature, plus more
      for greasing the pan
    1 cup packed dark brown sugar
    1 tablespoon vanilla extract
    6 large egg yolks
    2¾ cups all-purpose flour
    ¼ teaspoon sea salt
    1 large whole egg, lightly beaten

1. Preheat oven to 350°F. Cream butter and sugar in bowl of electric mixer until light and fluffy. Beat in vanilla and yolks one at a time, beating well after each addition. Add flour and sea salt, and beat just until combined. Do not overmix.

2. Transfer batter to a 9-inch tart pan with removable bottom. With small offset spatula, spread batter and smooth the top. (If necessary, chill batter 10 minutes before smoothing.) Place pan in refrigerator for 15 minutes.

3. Remove from refrigerator. Brush top with beaten egg, and mark a crisscross pattern with a fork. Brush again with egg. Bake until cake is deep golden brown and edges pull away from sides of pan, about 50 minutes.

4. Transfer to a wire rack to cool slightly. Remove cake from pan, and slice while still warm. Serve with Millix Farm Strawberry Compote.

Millix Farm Strawberry Compote

SERVES 4

2 pounds strawberries, stemmed and sliced
2 tablespoons Amaretto or Grand Marnier
1 tablespoon finely grated orange zest
1½ cups freshly squeezed orange juice

1. Combine the strawberries, liqueur, and orange zest in a small bowl. Toss to combine and allow to rest for 30 minutes.

2. Bring the orange juice to a boil in a small saucepan over medium heat. Reduce heat immediately and simmer until the liquid is reduced to ¼ cup, about 10 minutes.

3. Allow to cool. Pour the reduced orange syrup over the strawberries and toss to combine.

4. Serve with Patricia's Egg & Butter Pound Cake.

Patricia Millix

Pumpkin Paul's Farm

728 Merrow Rd., Tolland, CT 06084 | (860) 429-8449

Paul Peters is not your typical farmer. His farm stand lies at the intersection of Willington, Coventry, Mansfield, and Tolland in the Four Corners region of the Willimantic River Valley. The land that we know as Pumpkin Peter's Farm is all rented and leased, sans silo, barn, and picturesque picket fencing.

Paul has more than a full-time job acting as an agronomist, salesman, and technical advisor for growers throughout Massachusetts, Rhode Island, and Connecticut. He is a master of soil health and modification and integrated pest management. For him, farming has been an evolution.

Following in the footsteps of his famous father, scientist Robert Peters, Paul attended the University of Connecticut (UConn) with a notion of working as a farm manager for an existing agricultural operation, knowing that he had no real opportunity to access workable land himself. For lack of job opportunities, he set that notion aside after he graduated.

After ten years as an agronomist, Paul returned to his farming dream, finding the opportunity to rent and lease tillable land. Today he runs a part-time agricultural operation cultivating four acres of strawberries and a half acre of raspberries in Tolland and more than twenty acres of pumpkins on land in both Hebron, Connecticut, and Kingston, Rhode Island.

Pumpkin Paul's is a family farm, run with his wife, Stephanie Hawks, an accomplished educator, and his two daughters. In 2010 daughter Kara managed the harvest for the first time, returning from nursing school at Westminster College in Utah. Right off the plane, she traded a stethoscope for work boots. Joining her was Ada, who at sixteen managed the harvest of raspberries that Paul had planted for both sisters to be involved in before they played themselves silly in August—the last rush of freedom before returning to school in the fall.

Someone who believes in the value of goof-off and fun time, Paul is an avid whitewater canoeist, cyclist, and skier. Planting just strawberries and pumpkins allows Paul and his family the opportunity to enjoy their playtime together. Farming is demanding, and Paul clearly understands that. While there are many things he'd like to accomplish at Pumpkin Paul's Farm, he occasionally must leave chores undone to ensure good, quality time with his family.

"It is about balance in our daily lives," he says. "A lot of farmers are so focused that they lose their connections with their families. This is a family-run operation. We play together, connect together, eat together, work together, and will hopefully grow old knowing one another."

Tending to weeds or taking the girls canoeing? You'll find Paul prioritizing the nourishment and cultivation of his family relationships over his daily chores. Don't misunderstand: His farm is also well cared for and fruitful. Be assured that Paul can offer the best of both spring and fall crops in perfect balance with his growing children. Lovely.

Kara & Ada's Strawberry Raspberry Pie

MAKES 1 9-INCH PIE

Crust

> *9 graham crackers, broken into rough pieces*
> *5 tablespoons unsalted butter, melted and warm*

Berry filling

> *3 cups strawberries, rinsed and quartered*
> *3 cups whole raspberries, rinsed*
> *2½ tablespoons maple syrup, divided*
> *3 tablespoons cornstarch*
> *¼ teaspoon sea salt*
> *¼ cup freshly squeezed orange juice, divided*

> *Vanilla-flavored whipped cream*

1. Adjust oven rack to middle position and preheat oven to 350°F.

2. In a food processor, process graham crackers until ground fine. With the motor running, add melted butter in a steady stream, and pulse until the mixture resembles wet sand. Put graham cracker mixture into a 9-inch glass pie plate, and press into an even thickness around the bottom and sides. Bake until fragrant and just beginning to brown, about 15 minutes. Transfer to a wire rack to cool completely.

3. Combine strawberries and raspberries and pulse 2½ cups of the berry mixture in a food processor until smooth and fully pureed, about 1 minute. Strain puree in a mesh strainer into a small saucepan, pressing seeds to extract the juice. Combine 2 tablespoons of maple syrup, the cornstarch, and sea salt in a small bowl. Add to berry puree.

4. Bring puree to a boil over medium heat and heat, stirring constantly, until thickened to a consistency of pudding. Remove from heat. Stir in 1 tablespoon orange juice, and set aside to cool slightly.

5. Place remaining berries in a medium bowl. Heat remaining orange juice and remaining 2 teaspoons maple syrup in a second small saucepan until syrupy and reduced to about 3 tablespoons. Drizzle the orange syrup over the berries, and toss gently to coat. Cool slightly.

6. Pour puree into cooled pie shell. Top with fresh berries. Loosely cover with plastic wrap, and refrigerate until chilled and the puree has set, about 3 hours or overnight.

7. Serve with vanilla-flavored whipped cream.

Paul Peters

Paul's Curried Pumpkin Soup

SERVES 4–6

8 tablespoons plain whole-milk yogurt

4 tablespoons minced fresh cilantro

2 teaspoons freshly squeezed lime juice

½ teaspoon sea salt

1 small pumpkin, about 3 pounds, cut in half lengthwise and seeded

4 tablespoons butter

1 large shallot, minced

2 cups dry white wine

4 cups low-sodium chicken stock

1 teaspoon sea salt

2 medium parsnips, about 1 pound, peeled and quartered

2 teaspoons curry powder

¼ cup heavy cream

¼ teaspoon honey

½ teaspoon nutmeg

Sea salt and pepper to taste

1. Combine the yogurt, cilantro, lime juice, and ½ teaspoon sea salt together in a bowl. Refrigerate.

2. Cut the pumpkin in half lengthwise; and save the seeds and "strings."

3. Melt butter in a 4-quart stockpot. Sauté the shallot in butter until translucent. Add the pumpkin scrapings and seeds and continue to cook, stirring occasionally, until the butter turns orange in color, about 4 minutes. Add wine, chicken stock, and 1 teaspoon sea salt, and bring the seeds to a boil over high heat.

4. Reduce heat. Place the pumpkin and parsnips in a steamer basket, and lower the basket into the stockpot. Cover and steam until the pumpkin is completely tender, 20 to 30 minutes.

5. Remove pot from heat. Use tongs to remove the pumpkin and parsnips. When cool enough to handle, spoon the pumpkin flesh from the skins. Reserve the flesh and the parsnips.

6. Strain the steaming liquid through a mesh strainer. Rinse and dry the pot.

7. Puree the pumpkin and parsnips in batches in the food processor, adding just enough steaming liquid to obtain a smooth consistency and adding the curry powder while the blades are turning.

8. Transfer the puree back to the cleaned pot. Stir in the remaining steaming liquid, cream, and honey. Warm the soup over medium-low heat until hot. Add the nutmeg, and season to taste with sea salt and pepper. Serve immediately with a large dollop of the cilantro-yogurt mixture.

WINTERBROOK FARM

116 Beffa Rd., Stafford Springs, CT 06076 | (860) 684-2124

Laura and Kirby Judd are warm, endearing, and tender souls—easy to talk to and comforting in their company. Both former educators, these proprietors of Winterbrook Farm continue to engage in their community long after their nineteen years of service as 4-H leaders. Kirby taught sixth grade for forty-three years after graduating from Yale, Harvard, and the University of Connecticut. Laura, a double major in biology and recreation and youth leadership, taught at Springfield College in nonprofit management and environmental education. With a master's from the University of Illinois, she too thought she'd die in a Midwest winter, just as I did during my college days in Wisconsin.

Finishing their careers, they hobby-farmed in spring and summer until they retired—self-taught, learning as they went, and growing their operation every year. Today the Judds annually provide pick-your-own organic blueberries and peaches, maple syrup, and thousands of bales of hay. They are one of the larger producers of wool in Connecticut and, using rotational grazing, offer the very best of lamb for feasting.

When all four of their kids were in 4-H together, and realizing that the number of farm animals in their residential suburban yard was quickly exceeding the patience of their neighbors, they searched for farmland, the only search strictures being that the property had to have an apple tree, a brook, and surroundings completely devoid of any traffic noise. They found what they were looking for in 1977, and what is now Winterbrook Farm is stunningly beautiful.

Laura coordinates the Connecticut Blanket Project—collecting more than a ton of wool each year from Connecticut farmers and creating blankets that are distributed back to the sheep producers for their own use or for sale throughout the state. Sadly, the wool-manufacturing industry in Connecticut has become defunct. Wool from Connecticut farmers must be sent to South Carolina to be cleaned, to Massachusetts for spinning into yarn by commissioned weavers, then to Rhode Island to be finished—all shipped around by Textile Trucking from New Hampshire. Each year the Connecticut Blanket Project creates more than 275 blankets of the finest quality, stewarded in part by Laura's wool quality workshops for the Connecticut Sheepherders Association, which teaches sheep tenders how to preserve and create fine wool.

Neither Laura nor Kirby will ever retire from their second career as farmers. They're "heading off Winterbrook Farm feet first," she chuckles. Relying on friends who come to help keep the farm operational, these seasoned elders will produce our food until their very last days.

Grandson Cooper and a newborn

Winterbrook Farm is an open house, with doors ajar for blueberry pickers and maple syrup boiling. Still teaching, Laura and Kirby are mentors to the younger generation of farmers following in their footsteps, enjoying the sounds of grandkids canoeing across the pond as they sit on their screened-in porch during those rare summer moments of respite.

Farmer Kirby's Weeping Leg of Lamb

SERVES 4

> 3 teaspoons ground peppercorns
> 1 teaspoon cumin seeds
> ½ teaspoon coriander seeds
> 2 cloves garlic, sliced
> 3 teaspoons sea salt
> 2½ tablespoons extra virgin olive oil, divided
> 8 large beets, rinsed and wedged into 1-inch pieces
> 1 leg of lamb, with or without the bone

1. Using a mortar and pestle, mash all dry spices, garlic, and sea salt into a rough paste. Add 1 tablespoon olive oil, and continue working into a smoother paste. Add second tablespoon of olive oil to create a slurry.

2. Divide the spice paste, placing ⅓ into a separate bowl.

3. Lightly coat the beets with ½ tablespoon olive oil and place at the bottom of a roasting pan that has a meat rack attachment.

4. Take the remaining ⅔ of the spice paste and rub into the leg of lamb. Place lamb on a rack inside the roasting pan, over the beets.

5. With a bone-in leg of lamb (recommended), bake at 400°F for 10 minutes, 375°F for 10 minutes, 350°F for 15 minutes, and then 325°F for 30 minutes, or until the lamb registers 140°F on a meat thermometer.

6. With a boneless leg of lamb, bake at 400°F for 10 minutes, 350°F for 10 minutes, and then 325°F for 30 minutes, or until the lamb registers 130°F on a meat thermometer.

7. Remove lamb from the oven; tent with foil and allow to rest at room temperature for 20 minutes before carving.

8. Serve the sliced lamb and roasted beets with Winterbrook Farm Red Quinoa Tabbouleh. This entire meal is especially good with House of Hayes Spicy Peaches (See page 44.).

Note: This is called a weeping leg of lamb, or *le gigot qui pleure,* because juices from the roasting lamb drip down onto the beets, making them so much more flavorful.

Winterbrook Farm Red Quinoa Tabbouleh

SERVES 4

*⅓ cup spice paste, reserved from Farmer Kirby's
    Weeping Leg of Lamb
2 tablespoons olive oil
Juice of one lemon
1 cup red quinoa
1 cup minced mint
2 cups minced parsley
1 cup sliced scallions
Sea salt and pepper to taste*

1. To the spice paste, add 2 tablespoons olive oil and the juice of one lemon. Set aside.

2. Follow package directions to make 2 cups red quinoa—making sure that it has been well rinsed. Once cooked, remove from heat and allow to rest, covered, at room temperature for about 5 minutes.

3. In a large bowl, combine mint, parsley, scallions, and cooked but still warm red quinoa. Toss to combine. Add spice mixture paste, and stir. Season to taste with sea salt and pepper. Cover and serve at room temperature.

Chapter 8

WINDHAM COUNTY

❧

CRANBERRY HILL FARM

158 Nagy Rd., Ashford, CT 06278 | (860) 429-3923

Cranberry Hill Farm is a love story. Art Talmadge and Sherry Simpson both decided to go to school later in life. Prior to being a thirty-year-old freshman, Art had a full-time job in construction. When the housing market crashed in the late 1980s, he went back to school to study forestry and met Sherry, who had enlisted at the University of Connecticut (UConn) for a degree in horticulture. They fell instantly in love, and wedding bells rang.

Throughout their school years they sat, heads together, over the dining room table in Storrs, envisioning their dream farm. They still have their original papers, outlining their vision for their future in agriculture. And how did they happen upon a parcel of acreage of the original Nagy Farm?

Art had graduated, and while taking a break from his forestry duties in the company truck with a cup of coffee in a Dunkin' Donuts parking lot, he noticed an elderly gentleman getting out of his car. The man walked slowly and deliberately over to Art. They chatted for about half an hour, the gentleman telling his life story—out of the blue, two strangers chatting through a rolled-down window over a cup of hot coffee. As the man turned to leave, he said over his shoulder, "If you know a young couple who wants to buy an old farm, you have them give me a call."

Two weeks later, Sherry and Art pulled into the driveway. They knew instantly, without even seeing the rest of the property, that this was their dream; this was their farm. Cranberry Hill Farm was born. Art and Sherry have been farming for eight years on thirty acres—a small parcel of the original 600-acre Nagy farm created in the 1920s by the Nagy family, who emigrated from Czechoslovakia.

Selling heirloom vegetables and working on a maple syrup project with the Yale School of Forestry, Cranberry Hill Farm abuts the Yale Forest on two sides—about 8,000 acres of pristine woodland. They have hand-cleared and hand-tended their growing plots. Currently focused on vegetables and heirloom poultry, in the future Cranberry Hill Farm will include livestock such as pigs and cows, an expansion of their sugar bush, possible cultivation of cranberries from the bog, and continued involvement in the Last Green Valley's agritourism opportunities.

Sherry and Art have survived rebuilding the original house despite several moments of sheer panic—like the time an exhausted Sherry relaxed in the bathtub and realized too late that the pipes were no longer connected. Pulling the drain plug sent a torrent of water crashing through the ceiling and down into the living room. They survived an outdoor shower system for six

Art Talmadge and Sherry Simpson

Cranberry Hill Farm Cumin-Crusted Chicken with Cilantro Gremolata

SERVES 4

> 1 tablespoon plus 1 teaspoon cumin seeds
> ½ teaspoon sea salt
> ¼ teaspoon freshly ground black pepper
> 4 boneless, skinless chicken thighs
> 1½ teaspoons extra virgin olive oil

Gremolata

> 1 teaspoon finely minced garlic
> ¼ teaspoon sea salt
> 1½ teaspoons finely grated lemon zest
> ¼ cup coarsely chopped fresh cilantro (or flat-leaf parsley)
> 3 tablespoons extra virgin olive oil

1. In a small, dry skillet, toast the cumin seeds over moderate heat until fragrant. Coarsely grind in a mortar and pestle. Stir in the salt and pepper, and transfer to a plate.

2. Press the chicken thighs down into the cumin-salt mixture and rub until all sides are covered. Allow to rest while you make the gremolata.

3. Place the garlic on a cutting board; add the sea salt and lemon zest, and mince together. Add the cilantro, and continue chopping until finely chopped. Place in a small bowl and add the 3 tablespoons olive oil. Set aside.

months while the damage was being repaired. They survived the drilling of a well that led to no water. They'll survive much, much more at Cranberry Hill Farm. But these two newlyweds have a dream. Cranberry Hill Farm is stunningly beautiful. And they're happy.

4. Heat a large nonstick skillet over moderately high heat. Add the 1½ teaspoons olive oil and swirl to coat. Add the chicken thighs, laid out flat in a single layer. Sear for 1 minute.

5. Flip the chicken and sear the other side until well browned. Turn the chicken again; reduce heat to medium and cover. Allow to simmer for 5 minutes.

6. When chicken is somewhat springy to the touch, remove to a platter. Cover loosely with foil, and allow to rest for about 5 minutes to finish cooking.

7. To serve, sprinkle with the gremolata. Serve immediately.

Art & Sherry's Tomato Bread Salad

SERVES 6

4–5 fresh tomatoes, cored and wedged
½ teaspoon sea salt
3 tablespoons extra virgin olive oil
1½ tablespoons rice wine vinegar or mirin
⅓ cup chopped fresh basil leaves
3 anchovy fillets, rinsed and mashed
Ground black pepper
4 large ¾-inch-thick slices chewy country-style bread, toasted and cut into ¾-inch cubes

1. Toss tomato wedges with sea salt in a medium bowl. Let rest for 15 to 20 minutes.

2. Whisk olive oil, vinegar, basil, mashed anchovies, and pepper to taste in a small bowl. Pour over the tomatoes and toss to coat. Set aside for about 10 minutes to blend flavors.

3. Add bread cubes and toss to combine. Adjust seasonings and serve immediately.

Fort Hill Farms & Gardens

260 Quaddick Rd., Thompson, CT 06277 | (860) 923-3439 | www.forthillfarms.com

Kristin Orr is a spunky blond powerhouse with especially eccentric green sunglasses that seem oddly fitting. From time to time she calls herself the Little Red Hen, but she is also quick to acknowledge that chaos equals opportunity.

Emigrating from Penn State to live in Stonington when Peter came to work at Pfizer, Kristen started teaching exercise classes. Hating the traffic while the casino was being built, Kristen took to her shell and started rowing to work along the Mystic River. After a major collision on the waters—Kristen was run over by a sailboat—she packed up her oars and made a decision. "I got in my shell, rowed home, and told Pete to quit his job at Pfizer. We're goin' farming."

With original plans to build a nursery, Peter and Kristen began clearing their land, only to discover the remains of a barn and an entire walled-in enclosure. They had found their own secret garden.

In 1889 John Doane, one of the founders of the Chicago & Pacific Union Railroad, arrived in the northeast corner of Connecticut from Chicago with "a train load of money." He bought parcels of land from Lord Thompson's children, created a dairy farm, and called it Fort Hill Farms, after the Native American fort that once stood on the land.

With his steel magnate business partner, Doane imported Italian immigrants, paying them 5 cents a day to build extensive stone walls throughout the Fort Hill Farm property. These majestic walls, 350 feet long and 12 feet high, were found accidentally by Kristin. She began the long, five-year struggle to hand-clear the walls of oriental bittersweet and poison ivy. With

Kristin Orr

a pickax and sheer will, Kristen planted a labyrinth of more than 8,000 potted plants and 1,500 lavender plants at the base of these majestic rock walls.

Today Fort Hill Farms is a glorious sight. Still a dairy farm and a member of the brilliant Farmer's Cow cooperative, Fort Hill offers a corn maze that is beyond mind-boggling. Their ice cream stand offers the very best of locally made ice cream by Farmer's Cow members. Kristin's lavender is so high in volatile oils that it remains fragrant for years, should you wish to leave it on a shelf. It's also perfectly divine for throwing into your food.

You simply must come and visit. If you want to get lost, come to the corn maze. If you want to be found, come to the labyrinth.

Fort Hill Farms Lavender Spice Rub
SERVES 4

2 tablespoons white or black peppercorns
1 tablespoon fennel seeds
2 tablespoons dried lavender flowers
2 small cloves garlic
3 teaspoons sea salt
3 tablespoons fresh thyme leaves
1 tablespoon extra virgin olive oil
2 teaspoons maple syrup

1. In a spice or coffee grinder, coarsely grind the peppercorns, fennel seeds, and lavender flowers.

2. Using a mortar and pestle, pound the garlic and sea salt into a paste. Add thyme, and continue pounding into a paste. Add olive oil, maple syrup, and the ground spices. Mash into a thick, flavorful paste.

3. This spice rub works perfectly with 3 to 5 pounds of chicken, pork, beef, or lamb. Rinse and dry your meat, and then rub it all over with the spice mixture. Wrap tightly in plastic wrap and refrigerate for at least 2 hours, preferably overnight. Proceed to the grill, or sear the meat on all sides before roasting in the oven. Always allow meat to rest at room temperature for at least 15 minutes after cooking.

Kristin's Lavender Pudding

SERVES 4

3 tablespoons unsalted butter
⅔ cup packed dark brown sugar
3 cups chilled half-and-half
1 tablespoon dried lavender flowers
4 egg yolks
2 tablespoons cornstarch
1 teaspoon port (optional)
1 cup whipping cream, whipped to soft peaks

1. Melt butter in a heavy-bottomed 4-quart saucepan over medium heat. Add the brown sugar and cook, stirring occasionally, until the mixture bubbles and becomes lighter, 3 to 5 minutes.

2. Reduce heat to low and slowly whisk the half-and-half into the sugar mixture. Add dried lavender flowers and stir until the sugar has dissolved, about 1 minute. Slowly bring the mixture to a gentle simmer, stirring continuously but gently to not break up the flowers.

3. Remove the cream mixture from heat and allow it to rest for about 5 minutes to allow the lavender to infuse its flavor. Strain through a fine mesh sieve to remove the lavender, and return mixture to the saucepan over low heat.

4. Whisk the egg yolks in a medium bowl until creamy. Slowly whisk about ½ cup of the lavender cream into the egg yolks. Whisk in the cornstarch and port until completely dissolved.

5. Whisk the cornstarch egg mixture back into the hot cream. Return to a slow simmer, stirring gently but constantly with a wooden spoon until a few bubbles burst on the surface and the mixture is thickened and glossy, about 3 minutes.

6. Transfer the pudding to a bowl and whisk in ¼ cup of the whipped cream until incorporated. Gently fold in the remaining whipped cream until just barely incorporated and the mousse is light and fluffy.

7. Press plastic wrap directly onto the surface of the pudding. Refrigerate until cold and set, at least 3 or 4 hours.

Hurricane Farm

65 Kasacek Rd., Scotland, CT 06247 | (860) 465-9934

When Erica and Chris Andrews realized they were having a family, they made it a priority to have at least one stay-at-home parent. Chris, a renowned teacher in the public school district, and Erica decided to grow as much food as they could to supplement the grocery bill. When it came to raising animals, Erica was a vegetarian for more than ten years, disliking the way animals were treated, how they were slaughtered, and how they were dipped in chemicals before being shipped off to the grocery store.

Then, one Thanksgiving, Chris and Erica decided that they wanted to raise everything for the traditional feast and invite their parents. Needing to raise their own turkey, they boldly embarked on their first meat attempt. They loved it—communing with their family over a table laden with foods foraged and grown with their own hands and the sweat from their own backs. At that moment, two farmers were born. When they found the right six and a half acres of land in Scotland, Connecticut, Hurricane Farm was born into this world on a memorable day in 2008.

Erica and Chris operate a family farm, trying to be as self-sufficient and self-sustainable as possible. They grow a little bit of everything—including all their own meat, maple trees for syrup, and vegetables. They share their wares, offering a meat-based CSA subscription.

Once a month, shareholders pick up meat that was just recently harvested. As the summer months pass, lucky shareholders have access to nitrate-free bacon and ham, grass-fed and dry-aged beef, free-range chicken, and a heritage Narragansett turkey for Thanksgiving.

There is something quite special about this youthful couple, who are among the youngest farmers we interviewed, in both age and years in farming. Their inherent realization of our limited natural resources and lack of global sustainability has drawn these highly educated pioneers away from the glitter of Wall Street and out into dimmed stalls to collect freshly hatched eggs.

Chris and Erica have their doors open wide. They want you to come. They want to encourage you to grow as much as you're able, and they're willing to teach you what they've learned. Pulling out onto the dirt lane as dusk settles, with the smell of dinner in the air, I felt a deep hunger in my belly. I want to do this too.

I waved goodbye to Peter, Peter, Pumpkin Eater, the two-year old steer who grazes the lane between the calves and the pigs, keeping watch over all the pens and species. Sporting a long dog lead and a purple collar, he walked back and forth with me as I toured the farm and stopped to romp with the piglets. What a friendly fellow.

Erica and Chris Andrews with their children

Hurricane Farm Rendered Lard

Pristine pork fat from Hurricane Farm
Sanitized jars (I prefer pint-size.)
Coffee filters or fine mesh strainer

1. Chop the pork fat into at least 1-inch cubes, removing any meat pieces in the process.

2. Heat oven to 250°F. Place pork fat in a large Dutch oven or casserole dish. Cook for about 4 hours, stirring hourly, until the fat has rendered and the remaining pork pieces begin to brown, creating cracklings. (You may find it easier to render the fat on the stovetop in a large soup kettle, stirring often.)

3. Remove carefully from the oven and cool to room temperature. Filter or strain rendered fat into clean and sanitized jars; refrigerate or freeze.

Note: Lard is lower in saturated fat and has a higher flashpoint than butter, making it an ideal fat to cook with and use in pastries. It also adds a wonderful flavor to otherwise boring dishes.

Farmer Erica's Perfect Piecrust

MAKES 2 PIECRUSTS FOR 2 SINGLE-CRUST PIES OR FOR
1 DOUBLE-CRUST PIE

2½ cups unbleached all-purpose flour, plus extra
1 teaspoon sugar
1 teaspoon sea salt
¾ cup cold lard
⅓ cup ice water, more as needed

1. Blend flour, sugar, and sea salt in a food processor. Add cold lard by rounded spoonful, pulsing until blended. When all the lard has been added, the flour will resemble coarse meal.

2. Transfer to a medium bowl, adding ice water 1 tablespoon at a time until the dough begins to clump together in your hands. Add the least amount of water possible. Gather dough together and divide in half. Wrap each piece in plastic wrap and refrigerate at least 1 hour.

3. Roll out the chilled dough on a floured work surface and proceed with your favorite pie recipe.

Note: Work quickly with piecrust dough so that it remains very cold. Don't hesitate to put the dough back in the refrigerator at any intermediate step in your recipe.

Jean Palazz

PALAZZI
ORCHARD

EAST KILLINGLY, CT

PALAZZI ORCHARD

1393 North Rd., East Killingly, CT 06243 | (860) 774-4363

At first blush Jean Palazzi is an unassuming lady with long blond hair tied back in a braid and a shy but spontaneous giggle that rolls out and catches you by surprise. Don't let the T-shirt and calm smile fool you. Jean is sinfully intelligent and wise beyond her years.

The Palazzi Orchard in Connecticut's "Quiet Corner" has an easy, understated charm—not unlike Jean and Mark themselves. They purchased the apples-only orchard thirty years ago and have been systematically replacing the ninety-year-old trees with new ones so they now grow a diversified fruit crop that includes peaches, nectarines, apricots, seedless grapes, blueberries, raspberries, blackberries, and twenty varieties of apples.

Unique to the seventy-five-acre Palazzi Orchard is a 200-year old Charter Oak tree commemorating Revolutionary War hero Zacheus Brown, who died at the age of forty-eight on June 29, 1791, and his wife and children. The surrounding graveyard hosts settlement families from the late 1700s and early 1800s—many families whose descendants reside in the East Killingly area today. Jean and Mark carefully tend the five different foundations and wells built on the property, remnants of colonial times when homesteaders first settled

together at the top of hills. When the settlers moved down into the valley to work in the mills in 1895, this property was turned into an orchard.

Jean Palazzi has been farming her whole life, and her family has farmed Connecticut land since the 1600s, first settling in Woodstock as the first to lay down roots in that tiny town. Her father still farms in Wethersfield, and it was while selling her father's vegetables at a farm market stand years ago that she met and instantly fell in love with Mark. Love at first eggplant, they say. Jean and Mark were married more than thirty years ago and have been farming every since.

And in their spare time? The Palazzis have two very sweet and very shiny Harley-Davidson motorcycles tucked inside the farm stand. Now that the kids are grown, this seemingly demure couple straps on the leather and roars along the winding back roads side by side.

Visiting the Palazzi Orchard is an invitation to sit under the Charter Oak wiping peach juice from your chin, calmed by the gentle breeze rolling through the high grass as you enjoy a view of Massachusetts, New Hampshire, Rhode Island, and Vermont in one scenic, hilltop panorama.

Palazzi Orchard Apple Pumpkin Pie

MAKES 1 9-INCH PIE

3 teaspoons grated fresh ginger

1 teaspoon sea salt

2 cups sliced apples, unpeeled

2 cups fresh pumpkin, diced to 1-inch squares

2 tablespoons butter, melted

2 teaspoons ground cinnamon

1 teaspoon nutmeg

¼ teaspoon ground cloves

¼ cup packed dark brown sugar

½ recipe Farmer Erica's Perfect Piecrust (page 199),
  or 1 refrigerated piecrust

1 cup heavy cream

4 large eggs

1. Combine grated fresh ginger and ½ teaspoon sea salt in a mortar and pestle, and mash into a smooth puree. Set aside.

2. Preheat oven to 350°F. Toss apples and pumpkin in the melted butter with the cinnamon, nutmeg, and cloves. Place mixture in a roasting pan large enough to hold the fruit and roast until dry and soft, about 1 hour. Stir often to allow browning on all sides. Puree roasted apples and pumpkin into a smooth paste in a food processor. Add brown sugar and the ginger paste, and puree again.

3. Increase oven to 400°F and adjust oven rack to the lowest position. Roll out piecrust, homemade or store-bought, to fit a 9-inch pie pan. Bake pie shell for about 10 minutes, or until the piecrust barely begins to color.

4. Transfer pumpkin and apple mixture to a heavy-bottomed 4-quart saucepan; add cream and bring to a bare simmer over low heat.

5. In a separate bowl, whisk eggs until frothy. Add hot pumpkin mixture slowly, whisking gently and continuously to combine.

6. Immediately pour warm filling into hot pie shell. Bake at 400°F until filling is puffed, dry looking, and lightly cracked around the edges and the center wiggles like gelatin when the pie is gently shaken, about 25 minutes.

7. Cool on a wire rack for at least 1 hour. Serve with Stanley's Cinnamon Yogurt Ice Cream (page 45) or House of Hayes Spicy Peaches (page 44).

Note: This recipe also works perfectly if you substitute squash for the pumpkin. Our family favorite is butternut squash.

Jean's Apple Baba Ghanoush

SERVES 4

> 2 large eggplants, about 2 pounds, peeled
> 1 pound apples, cored but unpeeled
> 2 cloves garlic
> ¼ cup extra virgin olive oil
> 1 teaspoon sea salt
> 1 teaspoon pepper
> 3 tablespoons freshly squeezed grapefruit juice
> ¼ cup minced parsley
> Sea salt and pepper to taste

1. Preheat oven to 350°F. Dice eggplant and unpeeled apples into 1-inch cubes. In a large bowl toss eggplant, apples, and whole garlic cloves with olive oil, sea salt, and pepper.

2. Place mixture in a roasting pan large enough to hold the ingredients without crowding and roast until the apples and eggplant are browned and the apples and eggplant have released all of their juices, about 1 hour. Stir often.

3. In a food processor puree the eggplant mixture into a smooth paste. Stir in the grapefruit juice and parsley, and season to taste with salt and pepper. Chill for a few hours before serving.

4. Serve with crackers, sliced bread, or toasted pita chips.

WAYNE'S ORGANIC GARDEN

1080 Plainfield Pike, Oneco, CT 06373 | (860) 564-7987 | www.waynesorganicgarden.com

Wayne Hansen dries his garlic in the barn where the hearse and the old horses once were kept. Upstairs is the old laying-out parlor for Oneco's town mortician in the late nineteenth century. Of course kids being kids, they came to steal the hearse on Halloween. Wayne tells the story of an old town curmudgeon, who was not feeling particularly well, being awakened in the night to see the hearse waiting for him in his driveway. Such is the history beneath the one and a half acres that Wayne and Marilyn cultivate as Wayne's Organic Garden.

This farm has been certified organic since 1989. And, as Wayne says with a wink and a smile, "Growing organically is how I got so old." Before farming, Wayne was a small building contractor in Boston. He didn't think he'd farm as a living, but now he farms as a life. He wanted to move to the country and found a place with more house and less land than he wanted—the boardinghouse for the quarry that at the turn of the twentieth century employed more than 200 people, mostly from England, as cobblestone makers.

With just one and a half acres of his own property, Wayne rented additional land and started playing with farming in the late 1980s. He moved to the country thinking he'd get into small-scale farming and perhaps sell some produce to a few friends. Now Wayne and his lovely wife, Marilyn, are easily one of the most celebrated organic farming couples in all Connecticut. "I'm sort of committed to it," he says. "I don't know what else I could do with myself. I'm sixty-five. I'm too old to start another career."

An avid cook who loves to play in the kitchen, Wayne sticks to growing smaller crops such as potatoes, garlic, onions, and other less space-intensive foods that keep well into the winter. Never having graduated from college because he dreaded the thought of working indoors for the rest of his life, Wayne is someone you would wish for as your favorite uncle. Because he is witty, smart, talkative, wise, and quirky in a perfectly endearing way, I have yet to meet anyone who can find anything negative to say about this man. I bet he plays a mean round of poker.

Since retirement, Marilyn continues to work for the Connecticut Institute for the Blind and is a brilliantly talented knitter, seamstress, and basket weaver with great design talents. And it's just the two of them, operating Wayne's Organic Garden with barely a paycheck.

As for Wayne's retiring? "I can't afford to retire. I gotta keep working. I've never worked so hard in all my life. But, I drink raw milk, I eat local food, and I still enjoy it. When people come up and thank you—thank you for growing organic food—that makes all the difference in the world. That makes up for it. As long as I can keep going, that's all that matters to me."

WAYNE'S ORGANIC GARDEN
Oneco, CT

Wayne Hansen

Farmer Wayne's Spring Turnip Greens with Garlic

SERVES 4

¼ cup pine nuts, toasted
1 pound spring turnip greens or other hearty spring
  greens
4 tablespoons extra virgin olive oil
4 medium garlic cloves, minced
1 teaspoon orange zest
Sea salt and pepper to taste

1. Toast pine nuts in a small, dry skillet over medium heat, stirring frequently until golden and fragrant, about 5 minutes. Set aside.

2. Wash and dice turnip greens into 1-inch pieces. Sauté in olive oil until slightly crisp and tender, about 5 minutes. Add garlic and sauté, stirring continuously, for 1 minute.

3. Toss greens with pine nuts and orange zest. Salt and pepper to taste. Serve warm.

Marilyn's Celery Root Salad

SERVES 4

Dressing

    2 tablespoons apple cider

    1½ tablespoons Dijon mustard

    2 teaspoons maple syrup

    ½ teaspoon sea salt

    3 tablespoons extra virgin olive oil

    3 tablespoons whole-milk yogurt

Salad

    1 medium celery root, peeled and rinsed

    ½ medium tart apple, cored and peeled

    2 tablespoons minced red onion

    2 teaspoons minced parsley

    Sea salt and pepper to taste

1. In a medium bowl, whisk together apple cider, Dijon mustard, maple syrup, and sea salt. Whisk in the oil in a steady stream. Add yogurt; whisk to combine. Set aside.

2. Grate the celery root and apple using a food processor or box grater. Add immediately to prepared dressing; toss to coat. Stir in onion and parsley, and season to taste with sea salt and pepper. Refrigerate until chilled.

Recipe Index

About the Author

Emily Brooks is the revolutionary new face of the local food and sustainable agriculture movements. Founder of Edibles Advocate Alliance, Chef Emily nurtures social entrepreneurs who support local agriculture, sustainable farming, and sustainable food systems, and she passionately believes in changing the social norm toward agricultural sustainability and development through education and coalition building.

Emily nurtures social entrepreneurs and innovators to build local, living economies and to

- Construct local food webs and raise sustainable community food systems;
- Create sustainable businesses and employ sustainable marketing solutions;
- Connect their communities to the sustainability movement;
- Implement corporate environmental and sustainability solutions;
- Engage in local agriculture; and
- Utilize cleaner energy to reduce environmental impact.

Emily specializes in entrepreneurial training, sustainable marketing, workplace and community sustainability programming, and corporate sustainability and environmental education. She is the creator of Buy Local Connecticut.

She lives in Woodbury, Connecticut, with her dog, Lady.